Desert Raids with the SAS

Desert Raids with the SAS

Memories of Action, Capture and Escape

The wartime experiences of
Major Anthony Hough

by Gerald Hough

Pen & Sword
MILITARY

First published in Great Britain in 2021 by
Pen & Sword Military
An imprint of
Pen & Sword Books Ltd
Yorkshire – Philadelphia

ISBN 978 1 39900 722 1

Printed and bound in the UK by CPI Group (UK) Ltd, Croydon, CR0 4YY

FSC
www.fsc.org

MIX
Paper from
responsible sources
FSC® C013604

Pen & Sword Books Limited incorporates the imprints of Atlas, Archaeology, Aviation,
Discovery, Family History, Fiction, History, Maritime, Military, Military Classics,
Politics, Select, Transport, True Crime, Air World, Frontline Publishing, Leo Cooper,
Remember When, Seaforth Publishing, The Praetorian Press, Wharncliffe Local
History, Wharncliffe Transport, Wharncliffe True Crime and White Owl.

For a complete list of Pen & Sword titles please contact

PEN & SWORD BOOKS LIMITED
47 Church Street, Barnsley, South Yorkshire, S70 2AS, England
E-mail: enquiries@pen-and-sword.co.uk
Website: www.pen-and-sword.co.uk

Or

PEN AND SWORD BOOKS
1950 Lawrence Rd, Havertown, PA 19083, USA
E-mail: Uspen-and-sword@casematepublishers.com
Website: www.penandswordbooks.com

Contents

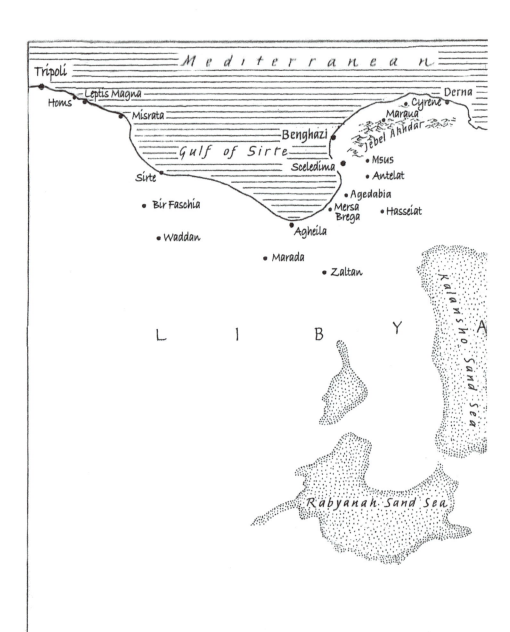

S e a

Tobruk

Buq Buq

Mersa Matruh

Capuzzo

Bir Gubi

Arabs
Gulf

Alexandria

Port Said

El Alamein

Kabrit

CAIRO

Isamailia

Qattara Depression

Great Sand Sea

E G Y P T

R. Nile

Red Sea

Luxor

A N G L O - E G Y P T I A N   S U D A N

Miles

0   100   200

Foreword

It is a great honour to have been asked to write a foreword for this book as Colonel Commandant of The Rifles. Here we have the remarkable memoir of a Rifleman who was a first-hand witness to a glorious but ferocious period in our regiment's history.

I was commissioned into the Royal Green Jackets in 1986 and was brought up on the exploits of men like Tony Hough who were our antecedents in the Rifle Brigade. I was also fortunate enough to get to know Tom Bird, of Snipe action fame, through my father as I graduated from a beater to a gun on Lord Howe's shoot in Penn Bottom. Tom's modesty was typical of what Gerald Hough captures of that generation and his father in particular in this memoir: despite knowing Tom for ten years through the shoot, it wasn't until he turned up at a Royal Green Jacket Snipe dinner that I made the connection between the Tom I knew and his image in the Terence Cuneo painting of that action that I had seen daily as a young subaltern! Tony Hough's qualities of dash and derring-do and quiet modesty are what we would all aspire to and underpin our regimental motto of Swift and Bold to this day.

When in 2007 our founding regiments formed The Rifles we made a conscious decision to be a forward-looking regiment that was firmly rooted in our past. Memoirs such as this one add to the fabric of our identity and we are much the richer for it. The campaigns of North Africa are of great importance to the identity of The Rifles and we wear them proudly as a battle honour to this day, commemorating the men of the Rifle Brigade, like Tony, and the sacrifices they made.

As you will read, Tony's experiences in the North African desert, a bloody and violent campaign, left an indelible mark on him, a mark that those of us who have seen the ugly realities of war will recognise as unchanging throughout the decades. It is a timely reminder to those that bear this mark that they are not alone and must share the burden which was foisted upon them.

I must also commend Gerald Hough for the manner and rigour in which he has brought his father's notes to vivid life in this compelling and fascinating book. It is a valuable and precious piece of history that not only pays great tribute to his father, but also to the courageous Italians who aided in his evasion and escape at great personal risk.

General Sir Patrick Sanders KCB CBE DSO ADC Gen
Colonel Commandant
The Rifles

Introduction

This is a true account of a young man's journey into manhood on the tails of the maelstrom that was the Second World War. It is also an important witness of one of the greatest chapters of that war in North Africa. The tale opens in 1940 with winter warfare training with the 5th Battalion Scots Guards, who were going to assist the Finns in their battle against the Russians, but the Finns entered an armistice with Russia and events moved on. Anthony Hough swiftly found himself in North Africa fighting a heroic holding retreat with B Company, 9th Battalion, Rifle Brigade. Retreat is one of the most difficult phases of warfare. The Battalion was decimated in hand-to-hand fighting. The horror of seeing so much death, especially of close friends and good men, is laid bare. Exposed is the anguishing futility of the ebbs and flows of war, meaning that months later after enormous slaughter one is back fighting in the same place. The constant changing of command led to the 9th Battalion feeling they never belonged. However, the 9th Battalion was involved in a series of military classics and the story provides many accounts of outstanding heroism and sacrifice.

Then in August 1942 after one and half years of fighting, the brave 9th Battalion was dismissed with hardly a thought. Anthony Hough and a number of fellow soldiers then joined 1 SAS in September 1942, wanting to see the campaign in Africa through to its climax. Much of what the SAS were doing was already what the Rifle Brigade had been doing and Anthony Hough fitted easily into the new regiment with many friends and with its much looser command.

Although the 9th Battalion, Rifle Brigade, was unlucky in its early deployment, Anthony Hough was fortunate, almost blessed. So many died around him while he survived.

In his new regiment he was reunited with some from the 1940s winter training with the Scots Guards, such as David Stirling and Carol Mather, and met many new 'originals', including Paddy Maine, Mike Sadler and others, and of course was reunited with men he had served with in the Rifles. After intense training with the SAS and in the company of such excellent men, it was incredibly exciting. Anthony Hough's summary of the character needed to join the SAS is well observed. The SAS was different, significantly by its lack of structure. Decisions were devolved to the lowest command of six-man sections. They were sent into battle with flamboyant disregard for survival; expecting that each section would find a way through, which of course many did. At the end of November, after their training, B Squadron, 1 SAS, pushed west and were deployed to the operational area between Tripoli and Bouerat, south-east of Misrata, in a critical stage of the campaign. Anthony Hough felt they were made expendable and it was clear that the chances of getting back were slim. Indeed, as it turned out, after a few weeks very few survived death or capture. However, their impact was significant.

Like almost all of the others in B Squadron on this December raiding mission, and despite heroic, selfless action, Anthony Hough was captured, after only a week or so, deep behind enemy lines and sent to an Italian prisoner of war camp in Chieti, Italy. The account of his escape in September 1943, his survival in caves in the Majella mountains, aided by the generosity and bravery of the local Italians, and then at the end of December 1943 in mid-winter breaking through to Allied lines is an epic escape and evasion story.

The book gives an insight into fear and how to control it, from the contemplation of battle to being depth-charged in an Italian submarine. There is an addiction to danger and the intense excitement of combat, but plenty of men were deeply and lastingly traumatised by their experiences. Despite the bravado and dash, the dark side of war and the effects of bloody fighting impacted on him as it did with many others. His great friend Major Mickey Rooney, from the winter warfare training in Chamonix, lived nearby in Essex and together, and with other friends, they helped each other talk away the horror. Mickey Rooney had an extraordinary career in 12 Commando, the Small-Scale Raiding Force, and the SAS. These local Essex war heroes were the inspiration behind my joining the Army and the SAS.

I was struck by the similarities between the SAS in the Second World War and today. The SAS are still achieving results out of all proportion to their numbers, frequently working deep in enemy territory, in small groups. Occasionally they will work in larger formation as shock troops to obtain a particular objective. Key elements remain: small four- to six-man patrols, taking a lateral approach, always seeking surprise and the unusual, and of course daring, willing to take risks.

SAS selection in 1942 consisted of walking very long distances with little food or water. Many failed. The selection process today is very similar, choosing the toughest and brightest and, each on their own, being subjected to days of long cross-country marches carrying very heavy loads, culminating in the 60-mile endurance test and still being able to think clearly. In the War the SAS only took about 5 per cent of those who volunteered. That is much the same today. What is being sought are the few that have individually the determination and skills to complete the tests. Most give up, but no one ever thinks the worse of those who do; at least they tried.

This account is an inspiring read and brings colour and realism to the history of this great conflict in the ghastly deserts of Libya. Gerald Hough takes us through the tale of his father's experiences in a sensitive, unassuming and perceptive way. As with many SAS men, Anthony Hough was a private, modest man and there is much which he kept to himself. He showed all the SAS attributes of fitness and intelligence, determination, inner resources of strength and resolve, good appreciation and planning, humility and humour. Gerald Hough's book brings out all these elements in the context of one man's wartime experiences. Ultimately, it is a rattling good story.

John Windham MBE, Captain (Rtd) Irish Guards and 22 SAS

Preface

My father talked only very rarely about the war, which was typical of his generation. However, over the years snippets of his story came out and when friends who had fought through the war came to dinner parties they occasionally reflected on their experiences over port and brandy after the ladies had withdrawn. As a child I would sit quietly at the top of the stairs listening to them, trying not to cough on the copious amount of cigar smoke drifting upstairs.

My father was an excellent golfer and a very good tennis player. He was charming, taciturn and rarely angry, and as we grew into adulthood immensely generous with his alcohol, which he enjoyed greatly. It never appeared to have much effect on him other than make him even more congenial. I remember at the wedding of one of my cousins he was sitting opposite me and next to an astrologist who believed in reincarnation. She asked him what he would like to come back as in his next life. From his wry smile I knew something good was coming and he didn't let me down. He said he would like to return as an alcoholic as he enjoyed drinking so much.

When my sister Alex came across the pencil-written account of his time in the SAS and his escape from Chieti it was too late to talk to him. It wasn't until my retirement from full-time work in 2016 that I began to focus on his story. The diary of his time in the SAS and his escape from Chieti was enough for me to construct the story. There was less on his early time in the war with the Rifle Brigade, enhanced by the letter he wrote in November 1941. I have written that period from chats I had with him, research and drawing on conversations he had with my siblings, especially my sister Alex Scott. My mother understood him deeply and gave me much valuable insight into his time in the desert. She was the one person he appears to have opened his heart to and luckily she had an unimpeachable memory. My journey to Italy galvanised her and we spent many hours together reaching into her mind and drawing out long-hidden knowledge, just in time as it turned out. He is also mentioned in various books and chronicles.

The highlight of my voyage of discovery was the journey to Pretoro and meeting the two surviving children of the Perseo family, the family that had firstly sheltered him from the Germans then kept him supplied with food while living in a cave near the village. I had struggled with how to write the book until after my first trip there. It was then that I decided to write in the first person. This opened it up for me. Maybe he was at my shoulder.

As I became engrossed in my father's story, I became more immersed in his time in Libya with the 9th Battalion Rifle Brigade fighting against Rommel's Africa Corps. What carnage it was as the two armies went forwards and backwards at speed, followed by backwards and forwards, and in the resulting mayhem many lives were squandered. The 9th Battalion got hit right in the gut at the end of March 1941. They relieved the 2nd Battalion two days before the Africa Corps launched its major offensive and after a heroic holding retreat lost half their men, either killed or captured. A year later the Battalion found itself back in the same place, but this time relieved a few days before the next Africa Corps offensive.

When reading the Rifle Brigade Chronicles at the Winchester Records Office I came across a submission by Sergeant Major Chris Collins who joined the 9th Battalion in September 1941 having been with the 2nd Battalion for the previous year. He recounts his time with the Battalion until it was disbanded and at its conclusion states the following: 'I remember on 28 December last we were getting shelled from a range of about 800 yards, and Major Baylay stood on, or rather just behind the brow of a hill, and as the shells were coming over us he was saying, "over to the right, slightly left, over the top", and acting much the same as if he were spotting for a trophy team at Bisley. I think he saved more than one person from a nervous breakdown, through his coolness; one other thing: he rarely takes cover from dive-bombing attacks until all those under his command are in their proper positions. He and his second-in-command, Captain A.D.V. Hough, are a shining example of all that is good in the leadership of their company, and I hope I am lucky enough to serve under either of them again, or else to get somebody as good.'

At the time he joined the SAS in September 1942, he had been away from England for 23 months and had been in combat for much of that time. When he finally got back to England in March 1944, he had been away from home for 41 months, leaving as a young 22-year-old and returning a man of 26 years and older than his time. As I write this, we are in the midst of experiencing a global epidemic called Covid 19. We have been loosely confined to our homes for eight weeks. People are fretting about the youth of our day losing their early life because they are restricted from socialising. There is plenty of food and the only shortage in the early weeks appeared to be toilet paper. I wonder how the men and women of the 1940s would view this.

This is his story, but it is also a story of the tenacity and bravery of the men who fought against a darkly satanic tyranny that threatened all free nations. I remember my mother saying to me that the First World War was a vanity war that should never have been fought but the Second World War was a fight against pure evil and had to be fought to its conclusion. Their sacrifice established a world order that has allowed our generation and those that follow us to prosper in a way that they could scarcely imagine.

My frivolous adoption of adult life after leaving school alienated me from him and it wasn't until much later that I began to understand him. It was only after his death and the writing of this story that I realise what a man he was and how accommodating he was of my superficiality. We had no comprehension of the war years in our youth and no understanding of the sacrifice so many made to give us the life we have had. I think our generation is now waking up to what the war years really meant, and for me this realisation has deepened or maybe uncovered the love I hold for my parents. It has been an awakening, and wonderful for it.

My paternal grandmother had three sons in active combat during the Second World War and she didn't survive the war. She died in 1940 from a cerebral haemorrhage and no doubt part of the cause was high blood pressure as a result of the stress she suffered. Two of her beloved children left England in 1940 to fight against tyranny and she never saw them again. Her children eventually returned home, but she was no longer there to welcome them.

My father was emotionally absent from my youth and I am now not surprised that he was, given his war. One can almost believe that there is a well of emotion one is born with and the war years had exhausted all that he had. He was a kind man though, and never a bully. He was courteous, good tempered and easy to live with, so I couldn't ask for more really. I wish that he had been able to share more of himself with me when we had the chance; and I had been able to think more of him than myself.

Chapter 1

Reflections

It is an unusually warm and humid day in early May in 1952 and I sit in my small office overlooking Victoria Wharf in Narrow Street, Limehouse E14. I have my windows flung open to allow what air there is to circulate. The whirring noise of the mill permeates the office bringing also the sound of trucks moving in and out of the yard and the general clatter of men at work. The air also carries the smell peculiar to cardboard manufacture that seeps uninvited into clothes and is hard to shed. I am unsure what it was that distracted me from analysing production figures, possibly the heat of the day and maybe even the sound of men at work, chatting loudly and ribbing each other in their strongly east London accents. Accents that take me back to my days in the deserts of Egypt and Libya when men under my command put it all on the line for their country. Brave, resourceful men from the Tower Hamlets who had fought hard in North Africa to repel Rommel's Africa Corps and with whom I had built a level of trust and affection that surpassed anything that I have or will be able to experience for the remainder of my life. Many of them never made it home and many others suffered terrible injuries inflicted by a brutally tough enemy intent on our destruction.

As I sit gazing at an unblemished blue sky, I ponder whether it is time to loosen the thread that has joined me to the British Army since 1938, a thread that is now threadbare. It has been important for me to maintain these ties to soften the horror of all that I experienced during the war. It has given access to a group of people who have endured much the same as me, allowing us to chat amongst ourselves with a degree of empathy not found easily elsewhere. However, in the intervening years from 1946 to now I have established strong friendships at my golf club with members who have shared many of the same traumas, coming away from the war with much distinction and award. They and ex-army friends living locally help to talk away the nightmare of dead and broken bodies that all too often invades my thoughts and dreams. Another reason is my growing family. My son Tony was born in 1949 and my second child will be born towards the end of this month. What with work and golf, rugby in the winter and tennis in the summer, it is becoming increasingly hard to find time for 21 SAS, of which I have been a member since January 1950.

My thoughts take me back in time, to before the war. At school I had been filled with a restlessness that was hard to temper. I played all sports quite well, learnt to box my way out of a corner, to shoot accurately, and greatly enjoyed the Combined Cadet Force, which I eventually commanded. I had been sent away from home to boarding school at the age of five so by the time I got to Uppingham I was hardened enough to stand up for myself. Early on a senior boy tried to force me to do something I didn't want to do and not only got a broken jaw for his efforts but he got a rapid exit from the school and after that it was plain sailing. I enjoyed the camaraderie of school life, the easy access to all types of sport and the subtle loosening of the reins as one got more senior. In my last year I was appointed House Captain and was able to bring a more conciliatory and empathetic approach to house life than was usual at that time.

Rather than move on to university in 1936, which in hindsight would have been more sensible, I joined the family firm and found to my consternation that life became very dull. The drudgery of the daily commute to Limehouse, the boredom of learning about cardboard production and most of all the inactivity preyed on my mind. On leaving school I had thought seriously of applying to the Royal Military College at Sandhurst but my father Harold had quietly persuaded me to give it more time and I feel he did so as the scars from his four years fighting in the Great War ran very deep. Initially he had been a despatch rider for the Marines on the Western Front but later in the war was commissioned and fought at Passchendaele, where he lost many friends and experienced a terror that I was as yet incapable of imagining. He and his two brothers fought with distinction and almost miraculously survived, with Alan, at the time a Captain in the Royal Field Artillery, receiving an MC. Growing up under this glamorous trio of warriors must have had some influence on my leaning towards the army.

Boredom and a growing need for excitement eventually got the better of me and in 1938 I joined the 1st Battalion Tower Hamlets Rifles Territorials, and once done I wondered why it had taken me a year since leaving school to do so, even with my father's caution. Amongst my fellow officers in the Tower Hamlets Rifles were a number of keen skiers, as I was. The battalion encouraged outward bound activity in training weeks and we chatted about organising something really extreme. I had been over to ski in Zermatt a number of times during my school days and considered myself to be competent enough to tackle most slopes. In early 1939 we hatched a plan to travel to Zermatt with the objective of climbing the 15,000 foot Monte Rosa with our skis either on or carried and finding our way down. What a challenge that had presented and I grabbed it with both arms. We journeyed out by train and fortunately were blessed with good weather during our stay. After a few practice days under the watchful eye of a seasoned Swiss Army mountain expert he signed us off as good enough to make the climb so early the next morning we journeyed up to Rotenboden and then skinned up and over the Gorner Glacier, eventually arriving at the Monte Rosa Hut. With great eagerness we set off at 4am the next morning and by 9am were about 400 feet below the summit, which was as far as we would go without climbing equipment. We enjoyed a long rest, relishing our hard-earned sandwich and hot soup, all the while taking in the fabulous view over Grenzgletscher and the Matterhorn. All too soon it was time to don skis and down we went, carving our way through deep untouched powder and picking our way through tight steep couloirs. It was pure exhilaration, dangerous at times, always the risk of avalanche, crazily fast with powder billowing out from just under the knees and utterly magnificent. It set me up very well for what was to come in February 1940.

With the outbreak of war in 1939 the Tower Hamlets Rifles was embodied for service in the regular army, and life changed dramatically. I had the impetuosity of youth to mask the horror of our country having to go to war again so soon after the last one, a war that had caused such enormous loss of life. I could see the sadness in my father's eyes as his two elder sons prepared for war and my mother Barbara was distraught. It was most likely that my younger brother John would also join once he completed his degree.

However, for me it was a welcome relief. Suddenly life was full. We went to Tidworth to train with the 2nd Motor Battalion, learning all the time, enjoying the challenge and hard grind of exercises in mid-winter and the comradeship found in the officers' mess. There wasn't much war going on in late 1939 so we had time to learn our craft and get used to managing men much more seasoned in warfare and rule-breaking than we were. Their library of excuses was worthy of the great fiction writers of the time and at times so amusing it was hard to keep a stern façade. I remember one joker who my sergeant told me had missed the last exercise, which included camouflage training. I had him brought before me and told him that despite his denials no-one had seen him on the exercise. Standing rigid in front of me and without a flicker of a smile he thanked me.

The Rifle Brigade was a motorised unit expected at times to be at the vanguard of the army, and even to operate behind enemy lines, so our training was very much focused on self-sufficiency and mutual reliance. We all had to have a thoroughly good understanding of mechanics as well as the normal learning of the art of warfare.

In December a notice was posted in the Mess that made interesting reading. The War Office was asking for volunteers with experience of skiing to join a ski battalion being formed as the 5th (Special Reserve) Battalion Scots Guards. I made enquires and while hard to extract meaningful information it was assumed that the battalion would be despatched to help the Finns and that we could be sent pretty soon as the Finns were engaged in a fierce battle with the Russians.

Chapter 2

February 1940: From a ski slope to the desert

The prospect of such an adventure greatly appealed to me, even though it meant me having to resign my commission and join as 'other ranks'. I stepped over the threshold of this unlikely battalion in early February and we gathered at Borden Camp near Aldershot. Dropping rank proved inconsequential as it appeared very few who had joined were not previously officers, as skiing before the war had been the preserve of the few. Our commanding officer was Coldstreamer Jimmy Coats, MC, who came with great credentials as an expert skier and a member of the St Moritz Tobogganing Club more commonly known for its Cresta Run. After the war he competed in the 1948 Winter Olympics held in St Moritz and came seventh in the skeleton.

After a few weeks of getting ourselves fit for skiing we were told we would be heading to France to train for two weeks with the Chasseurs Alpin in Chamonix. We embarked on the *Ulster Prince* at Southampton, which, with a destroyer escort, ferried us across the channel to Dieppe and there we crowded onto a train which took us to a small station at the foot of the Alps. I was amongst some very interesting and good fun characters such as George Jellicoe, David Stirling, Mike Calvert, Simon Fraser, Oswald (Mickey) Rooney and Carol Mather. We were determined to enjoy some serious high altitude alcohol consumption and be entertained as well as possible by the girls we would find there. We had enormous fun learning snow warfare and honing our skiing skills to perfection, which included the not easy task of carrying a heavy pack while on skis and to pull a laden sleigh with several other men. We also learnt all about survival in extreme conditions. Daylight hours in February were short so there was plenty of time to fully enjoy what was on offer in the village. We were young, fit and healthy so with that and the mountain air we found we could cope easily with the morning aftermath of over-indulgence the evening before.

We had adopted a nickname as the 'Snowballers' and it was all meant to be very secret but it became apparent early on that the Germans knew exactly what we were up to. After our two-week crash course, we returned to the UK and travelled by train to Glasgow, where on 12 March 1940, we boarded a ship that would take us to Finland. No sooner had we got our kit on board we were told that the unit would be disbanded as the Finns had entered into an armistice with Russia and the objective of our unit had gone. It had been fast, furious and great fun and brought me into contact with people that would become pivotal in my time in the army and after the war.

A welcome few days leave followed at home in Essex before I took up my commission again with the Battalion and tried hard to refocus on training for our eventual deployment to North Africa. When I reflected on the purpose of our unit, I was quite relieved we hadn't been despatched to Finland as it would have undoubtedly led to the loss of characters that played such a crucial role later on in the war. We were also hopelessly inexperienced for snow warfare in the extreme conditions we would have been subject to.

The 1st Battalion Tower Hamlets Rifles was destined for North Africa to join the 2nd Battalion Rifle Brigade, which had been operating there since early 1940 and enjoying considerable success against the Italian army. Much was going on in 1940, the evacuation of the British Expeditionary Force from Dunkirk as the Germans forced their way through to Paris resulting in the fall of France. I believe we were held back from leaving for North Africa for fear of the Germans invading Britain and it wasn't until the RAF had beaten the Germans in the sky that our orders came through to leave in November. I was boyishly excited by the prospect of battle, without any appreciation of how unpleasant it was going to be.

Under the command of Lieutenant Colonel Eric Shipton, with Major Joe McGraw as second-in-command, we boarded our new-looking troop ship in Liverpool mid-November and in cramped but comfortable quarters set sail for the desert. This was to be the first time this luxury liner had been used to ferry troops, and while it had been hastily converted to accommodate a couple of thousand men it still had an excellent supply of champagne, whisky and gin so the long voyage had first-rate prospects, assuming we didn't get torpedoed. The officers' mess was rapidly established in the first-class saloon and once the men had been loaded and settled in, we turned our attention to the bar, and it remained a focal point for six weeks.

During the voyage I established strong lasting friendships with fellow officers as we played poker and brag to pass the time while doing our best to consume the significant amount of booze on board. Tommy Meyer became a particularly good friend as we shared many interests and he had a wonderful sense of humour, accompanied by a booming laugh. He was deeply relaxed much of the time, sometimes to such an extent we had to prod him to make sure he was still alive. However, when he was able to rouse himself, he was decisive and filled with energy.

We firstly sailed west, deep into the Atlantic, zig-zagging all the way in convoy with many other ships and escorted by several destroyers. We then turned onto a south-easterly heading trundling along at a fair pace to minimise the risk of getting torpedoed by a German submarine. Occasionally a couple of destroyers would scoot off like excited terriers after a rabbit and the loud crump of depth charges exploding could be heard.

On the way south we pulled into Freetown in Sierra Leone but were not allowed to disembark. Fleets of canoes appeared from the shore filled with oranges and other fruits which we were able to pull up in nets having dropped coins onto the canoes. The daytime heat was incredible both on deck and below making life uncomfortable and unpleasantly smelly. It wasn't so bad for the officers, but the men suffered quite badly until we got far enough south for the weather to cool.

After a couple of weeks, we arrived in Cape Town, steaming in with the majestic Table Mountain standing behind the city, its trademark tablecloth of cloud rolling off its summit. Of course, we all immediately wanted to ascend it, and did so a day or so later. The mountain formed a spectacular backdrop to the many white painted houses with red tiled roofs rising from the shore. The local people welcomed us royally and we had a marvellous time bathing in the surprisingly cold sea, basking in the sun and attending cocktail receptions in the evening. There was a large tented camp available for us to use and the men were moved off the ship and given a chance to take a break from the monotony of the voyage. We had a week here without much to do, so with a few fellow officers I journeyed up to the Stellenbosch to enjoy the excellent wines produced in that region, accompanied by as much succulent meat as one could eat, something we had hungered after for over a year now. It was with some regret that we had to get back on board and into our cramped cabins to continue our journey to Egypt.

It was necessary on the next leg of the journey to get the men as fit as possible, so we conducted PT classes on deck two or three times a day, when the weather allowed. We also organised weapon training and some lessons in basic Arabic. As we approached Egypt our attention was drawn to the fight ahead, relieved to an extent by the fact that we had made the journey without being sunk. We steamed on through the Suez Canal, past the town of Ismailia, to where we were to return a few days later.

Chapter 3

Libya 1941: Our Baptism of Fire

We arrived at Port Said on 31 December 1940 and hoped we would be allowed to stay on board to celebrate the incoming year as we still had an amount of champagne to finish, but it was not to be. We disembarked during a cold and moonless night to have our first experience of the customs of the country. Despite it being quite late in the evening beggars besieged us on our march of about a mile to the siding where we were due to catch a special train to our camp. The train was special in the sense that it was extremely uncomfortable and with very little room. Sleep was impossible and we arrived at Ismailia on New Year's Day grumpy and tired, thoroughly fed up with having missed out on celebrating the New Year. As dawn broke, we had our first view of the featureless desert stretching away to the horizon in the west and which was to be my home for the next two years.

We learnt at our first briefing that action against the Italians was at its zenith, with the 2nd Battalion and others engaged in continuous combat. A senior officer whose name I choose to forget exclaimed quite pompously that the war in the Middle East was likely to be over by August. Ha! how often had that over-optimistic forecast been made in the past! The army in Egypt was commanded by General Wavell facing the Italian 10th Army of about 140,000 men. In December 1940 Wavell had ordered Operation Compass using about 36,000 troops and which had had spectacular success over a ten-week period, coinciding with our arrival in Egypt. In February when we were still mobilising, Wavell's forces succeeded in defeating the 10th Army and capturing over 130,000 Italian troops. This followed earlier success when Wavell's army secured Tobruk and Bardia, capturing 40,000 Italian troops. After this success, a good portion of Wavell's force was sent to defend Greece leaving him reliant on us raw recruits to fill the vacuum. In this theatre of war, we were a cosmopolitan army with troops from India, Australia, New Zealand, South Africa and Rhodesia. As the campaign progressed, I was to meet many of them and what wonderful people they were.

We had a great deal of sorting out to do before we were able to form up as an operational battalion, so the next six weeks were spent in a large camp near Ismailia, collecting our vehicles and equipment together and undergoing desert warfare training. It was quite different to the training we had in England as there we trained on roads or hard tracks and one wasn't likely to get stuck in a sand-drift. This period did give me time to bed myself in as a platoon commander and work hard with the men under my command to get them fit and ready for battle. We had heard that the Italians were hastily sending major reinforcements to Libya, bolstered by a German Panzer division under the command of a General Rommel. The word was that we would be pitted against these forces before too long and getting the men prepared for a long and bloody campaign was a priority. This was quite a challenge. By working closely with my sergeant, I established a strong rapport with the men, and they became akin to brothers in arms. I looked at them with the thought that within a few months many of them, possibly all, would either be dead, injured or captured. These were good men, mostly from London, some with experience in the army before the war. They really believed in King and Country and the need to defend our nation. It saddened me that such people should be faced with having their lives cut away from them in their prime. They were the bedrock of Britain and we could do without losing them in such a tragic way.

Shortly after arriving at the camp I was called in to see the CO who gave me very depressing and sad news. My mother Barbara had died in December from a brain haemorrhage. She was only 45 years old. It came as a shock to me as she had been so full of life when I left just a few weeks ago, hiding her concern and busying herself with making sure I had all I needed. She was very close to me, much more so than my father, who I found unapproachable, and had offered sage guidance through my adolescence into manhood. I felt particularly upset that I couldn't be there to help my younger brother Stephen cope with her loss, and he would feel it terribly. My brother John was in his final year at Cambridge so at least he would be at home and able to help. I knew my father would be incapable of showing any tenderness, as any empathy he might have had as a young man had been drained out of him during his four years fighting the Germans in Europe in World War One. I screwed up the telegram that Shipton had handed me and let it blow away into the desert, carrying with it my sadness at never being able to see her again.

In early February, the Battalion moved up to an area around Cyrene in the Djebel of Cyrenaica, where we spent a few weeks acting as policemen keeping the peace between the Arabs and local resident Italians. This area was quite fertile, and the Italians had established many residences, much to the jealousy of the Arabs. Once the Italian Army had been vanquished and in hasty retreat the Arabs had returned. It seemed very odd to find that on one hand we were fighting the Italians and on the other we were tasked with protecting them from our friendly Arabs. After a few weeks of this nonsense we moved to Benghazi, where we did much the same. Benghazi is a most attractive town settled snugly next to a brilliant blue sea. Here we were able to enjoy good Italian dishes accompanied by fine wine making the forthcoming prospect of battle difficult to imagine. We lived in luxury in abandoned flats close to the sea where we would enjoy wonderful bathing. The only reality at this time was we heard that German scout planes had been seen close to our front line 150 miles south of where we were, and the Germans were operating aggressive patrols, which suggested to us that an attack was imminent.

Our orders were to move south on 22 March to relieve the 2nd Battalion at Mersa Brega, which was now facing the Germans as well as the Italians, with the Luftwaffe beginning to play an increasing role in making life uncomfortable. With us were the Essex Yeomanry armed with 25 pounder field guns, one battery of anti-tank guns of the 3rd Royal Horse Artillery, a machine-gun company of the Fifth Fusiliers, two anti-aircraft guns and a field ambulance. I began to feel apprehensive now that we were making our way towards mayhem, with the prospect of being tested in a way that might leave me found out. It's all very well playing soldiers, but shortly the gloves were going to come off and I was to lead men into battle. I didn't feel quite as gung-ho as I had a few weeks ago.

We arrived to find a weary 2nd Battalion packing its bags for its journey east to enjoy some well-earned rest. We had a chance to catch up on their news and they had had quite a time of it. They had been in action since early September without much rest and had enjoyed remarkable success against the Italian army. When the 4th Armoured Brigade was sent across the desert to cut off the retreating Italian 10th Army south of Benghazi, it was the 2nd Battalion, with the 4th Royal Horse Artillery, that was sent ahead to cut the road south of the Italian force. This caused the Italians considerable surprise, as they thought the British were still 150 miles away.

The 10th Army was strong enough to completely overrun the Battalion facing them but lacked the will to press their attacks and that night Captain Mike Mosley took a patrol to the west of the 10th Army to fire at intervals from different positions to give the impression that they had greater strength than they actually had.

The next day the Armoured Brigade arrived from the north and the trap was set. The Italians realising this attacked the Battalion with some desperation. The Battalion and the RHA, against overwhelming odds, prevented them from breaking through. After several days of intense engagement, the Italians surrendered. It was a magnificent victory, in which the Battalion had played a crucial role.

A day or so later the 2nd Battalion collected its kit and left us, heading away to Egypt. Rather menacingly we spotted German planes flying over the area and it was clear we were soon going to be engaged with an entirely different and well organised foe.

At our briefings it was acknowledged that should the enemy attack we were going to be very hard pressed keeping them in check given the transfer of so many veterans to Greece. With this in mind the orders were to delay the enemy for as long as possible before withdrawing. To help us, there was an Armoured Brigade a couple of miles to our left which on closer inspection and to our consternation had the use of a number of captured Italian tanks. At first sight they looked in poor condition and were unlikely to achieve much even if they could get them working. On our right flank we were protected to some extent by the sea. We came to realise quite soon that this stretch of desert had many hazards such as salt-pans and belts of deep, soft sand, so making a rapid exit was going to be quite a challenge.

My company was echeloned back behind A Company and our forward defences were covered by marshy saltpans which we assumed were going to be impassable by tanks. The distance between our flanks meant that we were going to struggle to avoid being overrun. Shortly after 08.00 hours on 31 March the German and Italian army advanced, and both A and C Companies got a massive pounding from the air taking quite a few casualties. The Stukas didn't want to leave us out of the party so came over to give us a pasting as well, accompanied by low flying Messerschmitt 109s strafing our position. This was my first experience of aerial warfare and it was completely terrifying seeing our men have bits blown off them, vehicles exploding and burning ferociously, and the scream of a Stuka dive bomber giving warning of another bomb coming. It was surreal. A week ago I had been eating pasta and drinking wine sitting in a pretty piazza by the sea in Benghazi and now my whole world was being blown apart. I had to fight my impulse to dive into the nearest slit trench and lie there face down until it all went away. I forced myself to keep calm and issue orders to the men to pull in casualties and to ensure others got to the relative safety of the slit trenches.

We were not directly engaged with the enemy at this time and had a good view of what was going on.

C Company had been holding a rise called Cemetery Hill, a key strategic spot, for a couple of hours before being ordered back, leaving just one platoon and carriers to hold on for as long as possible. They were dive-bombed remorselessly and after a half-hour they too were forced to withdraw.

It wasn't long before A Company were faced with about fifteen tanks, armoured cars, infantry and motorcycles appearing over Cemetery Hill and moving towards them. The enemy tanks stopped out of range of our anti-tank guns, but the Royal Horse Artillery were firing from a distance and managed to score a couple of hits on the tanks which encouraged the enemy to withdraw behind the hill. The enemy had brought artillery onto the hill and were firing onto both A Company and our positions, sending a relentless barrage of shells onto us which meant lying in our hastily dug shallow trenches with the depressing sight of our armaments and vehicles getting hit and exploding into flames.

Despite this incoming hail of high explosives, I had to force myself to move in order to organise getting the wounded away from the battle area and prepare for the inevitable onslaught. At about 14:30 A Company was again heavily dive-bombed by a large number of German planes causing much destruction of vehicles and we supposed men.

We were ordered to withdraw and form a defensive line about twenty-five miles to the rear, so much of what happened next came from officers recounting the story of the unfolding battle. At about 16:30 hours, four enemy tanks and one company of infantry moved up the coast and attacked our right flank resting on the sandhills on the coast. Here were two sections of A Company and one detached platoon of C Company which had been moved back to form a flank. They were supported by a machine-gun section of the Northumberland Fusiliers. This little force fought magnificently, repulsing the attack with heavy loss to the enemy, and they continued to hold this position till dusk, the remainder of C Company being moved up again from reserve during the afternoon to cover this flank. At 17:00 the Battalion front was again very heavily bombed.

At 19:30 our right flank was again attacked by twelve tanks and strong infantry forces. The tanks engaged our positions with guns and machine-gun fire. Our anti-tank guns replied with some success, but by 20:45 hours enemy tanks and infantry were infiltrating through our main positions, and were soon well to our rear. It was now dark and A Company was extricated with the loss of one platoon and a further four vehicles. C Company in the right flank was got away save for one platoon.

The way A and C Companies held off these heavy attacks on our right flank, until dark, was a magnificent piece of work. They were in constant battle against tanks and infantry of much greater force, having at the same time to endure repeated bombing.

The enemy didn't press a ground attack on our weak position on 1 April, but again we had to endure being blitzed from the air with both Stuka bombing and strafing runs by Messerschmitts, suffering further casualties and loss of vehicles. The battalion casualty rate was very high, and our fighting strength was getting badly diminished. It was all happening quickly so there was little time to dwell on the loss of good men, men I had got to know and had trained hard with. At times I felt desperate and very angry. There was no sign of our aircraft to protect us, even though these dive bombers were apparently easy targets from the air. We got incensed at this as it felt as if we were expendable. As night fell, we had a chance to eat some bully, drink tea and snatch a few hours of fitful sleep, always on the alert for a night offensive. Exhaustion became a constant companion, only relieved when a Stuka arched its back in a dive or when a tank lumbered into view spouting flame and destruction.

I had been asked to lead my platoon on a scouting mission before dawn on 2 April and we located an enemy armoured unit some three miles in front of our main position. With support of another platoon we harassed the enemy preventing them from finding weak spots in our front line. We then radioed in a warning as we observed a strong force of German infantry unloading astride the main road running through our position, and once done we hightailed it back to our line. On arrival and after a debrief, we were ordered further back so weren't involved in what came next, which was the loss of almost my entire B Company. The inevitable attack began at 10:30 hours escorted by a number of tanks and the Battalion was ordered to withdraw. B Company's route of withdrawal was cut off by German tanks and they tried to drive out through salt-pans, in which they got stuck. At the time we thought they had been killed but later learnt that most had been captured.

C Company made our withdrawal possible with a valiant engagement with the enemy which resulted in many of them getting killed or captured. We withdrew north in a hurry to Agedabia but the enemy weren't letting up and by four in the afternoon engaged us with tanks and infantry. They drove powerfully into our defences, almost to our gun positions, and we had to stand our ground and fight hard to resist them. We were now fighting infantry hand to hand with bayonets fixed and it was a desperate, bloody affair. On they came and from our meagre defensive positions we repelled them.

Even with this valiant effort there were simply too many of them and I knew it was only a matter of time, and not much at that, that we would get overrun. Salvation came when our tanks made a short-range counterattack inflicting enough damage to make the enemy pause, opening a bloodstained window that gave us time to get away and retreat to Antelat, to our north. Here we regrouped and counted our considerable losses. Fortunately, we were left in peace that night and were able to get the wounded away east and some of the dead buried. As B Company now consisted of only about twenty men, I was transferred to C Company which had also been scarified, and we numbered about seventy men and five carriers.

We continued our retreat on 3 April leaving Antelat and moving northward to Sceleidima, which we reached at midday. The Battalion was ordered to hold the line from Sidi Brahim in the north to Sceleidima in the south. We struggled to find positions to build a defensive line as the ground was hilly and broken. HQ was moving further north and we had much difficulty remaining in radio contact but it became clear early on that we would have to continue our retreat, which we did that night until we came under the command of the Armoured Brigade and moved east to Msus.

The men had had little sleep now for three days and nights and had been constantly harassed by infantry, tanks and bombers. I felt exhaustion weighing me down and struggled to think clearly. It seemed just a matter of fighting a retreat against an enemy that kept snapping at our heels, constantly moving against us and wearing us down. A Company had lost ground and was several miles away from us and we had great difficulty with radio contact. They eventually caught up with us at Msus where we were relieved to find stores of petrol. There was also water from wells which was a blessed relief given we had another trek north the next day.

After an all too brief sleep we were up again before dawn and moving north, a hot tiring journey of forty miles which took until the morning of 6 April. We were able to get some desperately needed rest but all too soon we were again on our way until noon when we were ordered to act as rearguard to the support group at Bu Gassel. Fortunately we had no contact with the enemy and we were able to withdraw north-eastward to Maraua which lay on the main Tobruk–Benghazi road. Here we refuelled and the men slumped down hoping for some sleep, especially the drivers who were now falling asleep at the wheel.

It was not to be, and we were ordered to drive through the night and try to arrive south-east of Derna, a further eighty miles, by dawn on 7 April. I took a turn at driving one of the carriers when the crew slumped with exhaustion. We achieved our goal and more as we passed through Derna early morning. As we left Derna we climbed a long steep hill with many switchbacks which brought us close by the Derna aerodrome and it was here we discovered to our dismay that a small well-armed force of enemy tanks and infantry had taken a more direct route and had prepared an ambush.

We had a ferocious battle, with the Royal Horse Artillery anti-tank gunners knocking out a large number of their armoured vehicles and eventually clearing the road, but at great cost. The remnants of C Company and Battalion Headquarters suffered severely, and four officers were killed. To lose men who have become close to you is the most difficult thing to deal with in war. The deep bonds of friendship established over the previous year viciously cut from one's life. Even worse is to see it happen. One moment an active man full of energy entirely focused on the job and the next the limp carcass, often not entirely intact. It is shocking, deeply so, and the trauma of it lives long in the heart. Deeply scarred.

The remains of the Battalion reached Tobruk late that night where we were able to lick our wounds and count our losses. In eight days of a fighting withdrawal over 400 miles of desert we had lost 16 officers and some 350 men, 42 carriers out of 44, and nearly 150 other vehicles out of 200. I had lost half my platoon with eight men killed and the rest injured. It was the most awful feeling losing good men in battle and deeply saddening. Their characters, energy, humour and vitality all gone. Their families back in England scarred emotionally for the remainder of their lives.

I slumped exhausted into makeshift quarters and slept soundly for ten hours. The next morning an incomplete battalion headquarters was established, and one motor company was formed out of what we had left. I was left without transport, and with my few remaining men from B Company and with others also disenfranchised we remained in Tobruk, ostensibly to assist with its defence. The motor company left us to help with the outer perimeter defence of Tobruk, some eighteen miles to the east and where they were joined with other columns recently arrived from Egypt. This is the last I heard of them until we were reunited in mid-May.

I felt incredibly fortunate to have survived and I felt good about managing to cope with the stress of battle, and to be able to direct my platoon with enough assuredness to give them the confidence needed to fight on against overwhelming odds. We had been lucky early on to have been attached to the scouting party thus missing the destruction of our B Company and at this time we were not aware of the outcome, whether they had succumbed or been captured. Later on we learned that most had been captured. It is quite a thing to sidestep such a tragedy when it is your brotherhood that is affected. One feels guilt, almost as if one has run away. We hadn't of course. In fact our scouting party had at the time faced much greater danger, but even so it was hard to bear.

We weren't asked to do much for the first couple of weeks in Tobruk but this didn't stop me following with great interest what was going on in the city. News filtered through that Rommel had given command of the attacking force to General Von Prittwitz, who arrived outside the city on 10 April. The Italians had left behind a good defensive perimeter about eight miles from the port and the Australian 9th Division under General Morshead had spent their time well reinforcing the line. In fact two brigades of this division had been retreating with us into Tobruk, having been sent south to bolster our defence against the Africa Corps.

Morshead had about thirty thousand troops in Tobruk and a decent amount of armour. There were a few squadrons of Hurricanes to harass the enemy aircraft which took a keen interest in pulverising the port.

Von Prittwitz launched his attack almost immediately on 10 April and from all accounts he and Rommel expected a limited defence due to the expected rapid extraction of our forces by sea. He met the Royal Northumberland Fusiliers supported by the 51st Field Regiment who together repulsed the attack, killing Von Prittwitz in the process. A second attack came at us the next day from the south and this time it was the Australians who pushed them back. After drawing breath for a couple of days another attack was launched and that night I gather there was hand to hand fighting at a point in the defensive perimeter and the Germans forced a breach. However, to much cheer it appeared that Morshead had anticipated this and had led them into a well-planned trap. Using artillery and tanks he initiated a major bombardment on the attacking Panzer regiment inflicting a loss of seventeen tanks in the space of an hour or so. This gave us all huge encouragement after the weeks of being pummelled by this well organised, tough enemy. I had a better understanding now why the French and the British Expeditionary Force were so badly mauled in the defence of France.

Rommel was tenacious and over the next few days attacks continued with no result other than our capture of a number of Italian troops. Things then quietened down, although I heard that Morshead had taken the fight to the enemy with some daring attacks on which several hundred more Italians were captured.

All this was happening along the perimeter and much of what I learnt was third-hand. After the last skirmish things got closer to home with major raids by enemy aircraft, sometimes with up to fifty Stukas attacking in a group and other times lone bombers appearing one after another. I became quite blasé at this time and stood watching the attacks, trying to predict where the bombs would fall.

Not much happened in the town other than these frequent bombing raids and on the perimeter. It seemed Rommel had dug in for a siege, targeting strategic assets with his artillery. We were told that we would be shipped out mid-May by destroyer to re-join the remnants of our battalion and when the day came it was with a joyful heart and great relief that I left.

As we pushed our way eastwards through the sparkling Mediterranean, I reflected on the last two months and how much I had changed. While a few months ago I thought I knew it all, I now knew that in fact I had known very little. I also knew I had much more to learn and was bloody lucky to be alive.

After our catastrophic baptism we could no longer operate as a battalion and we were withdrawn into Egypt to re-form. Our location was at a place called Qassasin, about seventy-five miles from Cairo on the Port Said-Suez road. Qassasin was no holiday camp. It was a dry, dusty place surrounded by endless desert, very hot during the day and cold at night. However, it had a well-stocked mess, a tented cinema and adequate supplies of food and water, and best of all it was out of range or interest from enemy bombers and fighters.

I was told that B Company was to be re-formed so with the remaining troops and officers we created the core as we rested at the camp. Tommy Meyer was transferred into our small company at this time and we were able to spend as much time as possible in the mess consuming large amounts of whisky, playing cards and trying hard to cleanse the images of death from our minds.

Whereas physically we recovered our strength quickly, we were emotionally tortured souls and exhausted from it. We had seen the most terrible things happen to our companions and friends, men of extraordinary strength, courage and commitment, suffer awful deaths. Limbs blown away, guts spilled onto the desert sand, cries of agony as men burnt inside a tank and many injuries so awful that lives would be forever shattered. The men's faces reflected the ghosts of the friends they had lost, and you could see in their eyes that they had changed into different beings, forever damned to be troubled by the horror of it all. But they still joked and ribbed each other, chatted about other things, talked of how much they had achieved against a strong enemy. Slowly you could see them rebuild their conviction that this was a fight we had to endure and win, if only to make the sacrifice of others in our battalion worth something. Their resilience and humour picked me up in an unexpected way. I looked at them differently. Gone were the mischievous pranksters or the less than diligent. They had been tried and tested in battle and had proved to themselves that they were able to cope. They had done some extraordinarily brave things to help others and under terrific bombardment had kept their heads and fought back.

My relationship with them was therefore quite different. We understood each other and had established a deep bond of affection and respect. They looked at me quite differently too. Gone was the slightly self-conscious young platoon commander, replaced by a person they knew they could rely upon to lead with a cool head.

One in particular comes to mind all these years later. Rifleman Handscombe, who was a young man from the Tower Hamlets joining the Battalion at the outbreak of the war. As we neared engagement with the enemy, he became more and more skittish and appeared very nervous, almost panicky. He behaved badly and was brought before me a couple of times for reprimand. This began to have an effect on the other men but there was little we could do other than offer encouragement and not come down too hard on him.

When the enemy started their major push against us, foreshadowed by ferocious dive bombing by Stukas, he turned to jelly, cowering in a slit trench and shaking like a leaf. Through some judicious use of east London dialect his corporal got him up and engaged in the fight, though I doubt very many of his bullets were a threat to anything other than Bedouin graves. Slowly though, as the fight intensified and we started to take serious casualties, some of whom were close friends of his, things began to change. Rather than cower he started to take the fight to the enemy, firing with more precision and placing himself in danger by helping his comrades. As we started one of the many withdrawals with German infantry snapping at our heals, his carrier driver was hit by a bullet and severely injured. The truck was then hit by a shell causing it to catch fire and killing the three other men in it at the time. He ran from the passenger side under intense fire from the enemy, pulled the driver out and ran with him over his shoulder until reaching another carrier, all the time the ground and air around him being peppered with bullets.

After that he became a changed man. He developed into a brave and resourceful soldier much respected by his platoon and NCOs. Later on he would join my section in the SAS and I would not have asked for anyone braver to stand alongside me.

Towards the end of May we had an infusion of officers and NCOs from the 2nd Battalion and more riflemen came to join us recently arrived from England. These additions brought us back to full company strength. Captain Bing Baylay (shortly promoted major) joined us as our new company commander and I met our replacement company sergeant major, Mike Collins. Bing was a really good chap; congenial, supportive and at times very amusing. I was to find out later just how relaxed he was under fire. Collins was everything one would want from a CSM, kindly with a natural authority and ferocious if stoked up. He too was to prove as solid as a rock when in combat. He had seen much action over the previous twelve months with the 2nd Battalion and had all the experience we needed for such a pivotal role. I had been promoted to captain in April and became Bing's number two a few weeks after he joined us. It was at this time we were renamed the 9th Battalion (Tower Hamlets Rifles).

Becoming Bing's number two changed my life considerably. In the event that Bing was killed or wounded in battle I would be expected to assume command of the Company until a replacement was found. I was responsible for organising the administration of the company and a host of other duties. My life became very busy and after a week or so of getting used to it I began to quite enjoy the added responsibility. It also brought me closer to the heart of planning both strategically and organizationally and made things much more interesting. Tommy Meyer had become a good friend and confidante. He was a chap with whom I could have a good laugh with over a beer as he had a quick sense of humour. He was able to bring an entertaining slant on some of our exploits against the enemy, making him very popular in the Mess. In battle, however dire our situation, he would be able to come up with an amusing aside or anecdote. I remember one when we were awaiting our fate facing the full might of the Africa Corps in one of those eerie periods of tranquillity before the metal storm broke. He wandered up to me and recounted a tale he had heard from one of the recently added lieutenants who had served under Colonel Purdon, our soon to be commander, in a previous company. He had been driving out of difficult soft sand country and came across him very red faced as his sergeant tried to extract his vehicle from the sand. He stopped and rather stupidly asked Purdon if he was stuck. No said Purdon, you are, and handed him the keys.

During this interlude, the Germans had continued to focus attention on Tobruk and were laying a siege. It was critical for Rommel to take Tobruk as this would allow him to supply his army from a forward port which he needed for his major thrust into Egypt. By all accounts our naval forces were suffering severely in keeping the garrison supplied, and our airplanes within the perimeter had been largely destroyed, leaving free rein for the German bombers.

We were briefed that once our strength had been increased back to a full battalion, we would join the 2nd Battalion in holding the Germans from breaking into Egypt. There had been a couple of unsuccessful attempts to relieve Tobruk during the summer months but again our tanks were proven to be lamentably under-gunned in comparison to the German tanks. What was called the 'June' attack took place and was repelled, leaving Tobruk entirely reliant on the Navy for their supplies.

Towards the end of June, we left Qassasin and moved to a camp sited in the shadows of the Pyramids of Giza. This had the advantage of being close to Cairo, enabling us to enjoy its delights at weekends. We got replacement vehicles and were able to begin training in the Mena desert. It was here our new battalion commander arrived, Colonel D.J. (Squeak) Purdon whom Collins held in great esteem having served under him previously. Once Purdon was in place our training became more rigorous and intense and we started to learn about column work. The main objective of columns was to supply information gained by night reconnaissance patrols and in the case of the artillery to harass the enemy by day. As time passed the horror of April receded and we thought more of the future, establishing firm friendships and continuing to build our new-found mutual trust and respect with the men.

We remained here until late September when we were again placed under overall command of the 201st Guards Brigade and sent forward to take over from the 2nd battalion, which at the time was just east of Mersa Matruh at a place called Gerawla. Here we undertook extensive patrols right into the heart of the enemy and sometimes through and behind them. The patrols were exhausting as the officers were required to go out three nights in four and we had to get close to the enemy in order to collect vital data on minefields and dispositions. A patrol required us to drive some eight to ten miles in the dark across the desert on a compass bearing and speedometer reading and then a two to three mile march on a compass bearing checked by pacing. Once close enough to the enemy we would gather data about their dispositions and lay some mines. Occasionally we would come dangerously close to enemy patrols or sentry positions but usually were able to silently withdraw in the darkness. Patrols having direct contact and a firefight would invariably get into difficulties and some or all would not return.

Once we had as much information as we could get, we would retrace our steps on a bearing to the trucks and drive back in the dark to our lines. We had to get back before daybreak otherwise would be exposed to air attack. The information we collected was by all accounts very well received by HQ as it gave details of infantry dispositions, minefields and positioning of main armaments. There were times we were so close to the enemy we would be crawling between two defensive posts.

All the time we were faced with dealing with the dreaded mine, and so many of them, sown by both our side and the Axis. The Germans had a really nasty one called the S-mine, or shrapnel mine. When triggered it would jump out of the ground to about four and a half feet then drop a foot before exploding, sending ball bearings at very high velocity in all directions. Anyone within fifty yards could be injured. They were easy enough to disable once discovered but discovery wasn't always easy. The Italians invented their own nasty one which was encased in a wooden box so that our detectors wouldn't pick up the metal signal. We lost a fair number of men to these devices, either with their losing their feet or legs or being killed outright. There were thousands of mines used as defensive measures to force attacking forces into a narrow channel and they were a constant dread.

We had no significant major engagement with the enemy during this time, and those of us who had survived the intense fighting in April found this comparatively gentle rebreaking-in was a great help to morale.

I became much more confident about my role and my personal welfare almost became incidental. We still had to bear the will-sapping strain of an occasional dive-bombing raid and Bing Baylay displayed such panache you would think he was walking the dog on the beach. Our sentries were very alert to these raids and would pick up approaching aircraft a minute or so from bombs dropping. Bing and I would make sure the men were in their dugout before we too took cover. We would do so displaying an indifferent façade, even though the stomach was churning. Our vehicles would be spread out over the surrounding desert which helped to limit the amount of damage done. Invariably these raids took casualties, but surprisingly few.

Our night patrols continued and on one fateful night Tommy Meyer and his sergeant, Mayers, failed to return. We were told by those who got back that they stumbled in the dark into an enemy patrol and there was quite a firefight even though no-one was quite sure what they were shooting at. Tommy was seriously wounded at a time the platoon was withdrawing rapidly, in very close contact with the enemy, and his sergeant turned to try and pick him up but was overwhelmed. I later learned that Tommy had died of his wounds. We had had several months to recharge our emotional batteries and Tommy's death showed me just how fragile that battery was. I knew I was going to have to find a way of locking that part of me away otherwise it would dominate me and I would not survive it mentally. It was just incredibly sad to lose a very good friend and made me feel that it was inevitable that my turn would come in time.

Life in the desert is a healthy one even though we lived mostly on bully beef and biscuit. Water was scarce most of the time and we had to be clever with its use. We would cut a used petrol can in half and punch small holes in its base, over which we would lay a cloth. On this we would lay a few inches of sand. We would share water for washing and rotate who went first. After a wash and a shave, the water would be filtered through the can, coming out crystal clear and ready for the next person. We could keep water rotating this way for several days before it became foul. Rather than discard it, it was then used to top up the vehicle radiators.

The desert sand is hard to sleep on, and other than in the summer months, when the heat can become unbearable, it can be very cold at night, although pleasant during the day. There was more often than not a cooling breeze which would fall away around midday making it uncomfortably hot for a few hours. The worst of it was the arrival of the dreadful *khamseen*, most usually in the spring. The khamseen is a very hot wind coming from the south and it inflicts terrible hardship on all. It blows down tents, fills every crevice with sand particles, prevents any cooking, and irritates the skin leaving it in a raw state. It is impossible to see more than a few yards, and after a while it completely exhausts the body and mind. This greenish-yellow sand sticks to every inch of sweating skin, clogs hair and fills nostrils and ears. It would invade our food supplies and worst of all clog the air-filters on our vehicles with devastating effect.

Sand was also our worst enemy when it came to keeping our weapons functioning, and the men had the task of constantly cleaning all equipment.

We had a fair number of cases of sandfly fever and a few outbreaks of jaundice but neither were material. What was the real scourge was a form of blood poisoning from 'desert sores'. For those prone to it even sunburn could trigger an attack and it was difficult to shift. I was fortunate and didn't get any of these ailments. The desert was full of life and most of it unpleasant. Flies were a perpetual annoyance and existed in enormous numbers, there were scorpions, fleas, lizards and ants. The scorpions climbed into bedding and boots and had a very nasty sting which could easily become infected.

Mostly the desert is hard sand, covered sometimes with scrub, sometimes with stones, which can vary in size from small pebbles to large boulders. It is easy to drive across and we were able to use Arab graves as navigation markers and they are plentiful. There is an incredible beauty in the desert, especially at night under the brilliance of the Milky Way. It has a mesmerising clarity which I have never found elsewhere. During the day the escarpments, together with other physical features such as depressions, tablelands, hills and spurs, give a fair amount of variety to the scenery.

Chapter 4

Helter-Skelter into battle

In late October news filtered through that we were going to be part of a major attack against the enemy and in early November we were pulled back for a few days rest and preparation. It was at this time I wrote a letter to my father, believing that possibly it would be the last time he would ever hear from me and this is what I wrote:

9ᵗʰ Battalion The Rifle Brigade.
M.E.F.
1/11/41.
Dear Daddy,

Thank you very much for your postcards – I am afraid some of my P.Cs may have gone astray possibly, as I generally write once a fortnight. I am still very well and having as good a time as can be expected. I am not really certain how much one can write about the retreat from Benghazi. There's very little to it really except that we had three days hard fighting with the Jerry and then were forced to withdraw. I believe the distance was about 400 miles as we were 150 miles forward of Benghazi at the time. Our losses, which numbered about 400 in all, mostly prisoners, were caused by companies being cut off. As on the whole we were a fairly small force and our flanks were very exposed.

The Armoured Brigade consisted in actual fact of ourselves with support from 25 pounder guns and anti-tank guns, and 54 extremely ill-conditioned tanks, 25 of which were old Italian M.13s. The tanks were well to the south and in actual fact only six of them fought the Germans at all. These did quite well, scoring 14 hits on German tanks, but few out of the six survived. The remainder spent their time in trying to go, and all except four had to be burnt after the first 200 miles and never joined battle at all.

We are still uncertain of the size of the German force against us, but I believe it was a Panzer Colonial Division of about 15,000 men and about 500 tanks. We held them up for three days and then it was a question of clearing out, as they were by then all round us. So we went and didn't stop until Tobruk. I spent about six weeks in there and then came out by sea. During the show our air force was negligible, and we were dive bombed a fair amount. In Tobruk itself I witnessed some annoying bombing raids and became quite expert at telling how far away the bombs were going to land. The planes used to fly fairly low and you could see the bombs leave.

Now the whole situation is altered and we hope to have our revenge sometime. Next time I write I will let you know about a good battle we had at Derna on our retreat, when we were cut off there by a small but strong force of Germans.

I hope the business and everything at home is going well.

My love to all.

From Anthony.

Information continued to filter through about the impending attack and it seemed the whole of the recently formed Eighth Army was going to be involved in a major push against the German positions in an attempt to lift the siege of Tobruk. Our job was to be held in reserve and protect the supply dumps should the Germans counterattack. It was also envisaged that we would at some point make a dash across the desert to cut off the enemy on the Gulf of Sirte, but circumstances arose which prevented it ever being put into action.

We knew we had an acute disadvantage against German tanks, which were capable of knocking out any armoured vehicle of ours from two thousand yards. The maximum effective range of our tank's 2-pounder guns was six to eight hundred yards. The only method we had of knocking out enemy tanks was the use of 25-pounder field guns firing over open sights. These guns would more usually be used to fire long distance, possibly as far away as ten miles, and there was no protection for the gun crews.

Rommel appeared to have other ideas about our relief of Tobruk and had his own plans to drive into Egypt. On 18 November we received the order to move 100 miles with speed to a place called Bir Gubi, about 70 miles into Libya, where we engaged the enemy in a series of skirmishes.

News that Rommel had made a break through meant we were ordered to turn tail and make haste back to defend the supply dumps and for a time we were travelling parallel to the German advancing forces. Fortunately, they missed the supply depot and charged on, no doubt looking forward to tea in Cairo.

Having got back to the dumps we were ordered to immediately cut off and repel 50 German tanks and infantry moving close by to where we were. This was a worrying prospect as we had limited armour. In what was later labelled the 'November Gold Rush' we were presented with a most gratifying spectacle. We were about twenty miles to the west of Capuzzo and tentatively feeling our way towards this overwhelming enemy force to engage in what would be a decimating battle. Yet again we were being faced with the destruction of the Battalion but what choice did we have, we had to slow them down otherwise Rommel would get to Cairo and the chaps in HQ might be exposed to the sharp end of war.

The Germans decided to take us on and began to advance towards us and it was then that a couple of squadrons of RAF bombers roared overhead and dropped their bombs causing quite a bit of damage. The advance stopped but after a while they sorted themselves out and began to move towards us again. We then spotted about fifty Stukas coming in our direction so assumed we were in for a pasting. Much to our astonishment the Stukas circled their own tanks and troops and with great precision dived and released their bombs one after another, causing considerable destruction. I watched this with some disbelief and found myself waving them on with a great deal of enthusiasm. The Stukas circled above the tanks like a flock of pelicans circling its underwater prey. As a Stuka picked its targets, it would turn into a steep dive with wings that looked similar to the pelican as it launched itself downwards into the sea. The plane would drop with alarming speed and ferocity emitting that dreadful wail of impending doom, release its bomb with now pleasing accuracy and then climb away leaving destruction in its wake. It was unusual for me to be able to observe this as a spectator and most gratifying it was! Once they had unleashed all they had they happily buzzed away west and soon were out of sight. At this point the German tank regiment must have felt thoroughly fed up and in considerable distress but their trial was not yet over. No sooner had the Stukas faded out of sight our bombers reappeared, unloading several more tonnes of high explosives, and what remained of the Germans after this clearly felt that enough was enough and hightailed it back towards their own line. The carnage left behind, smoking and burning furiously in the evening light, was a most satisfying sight.

We re-joined the 201st Guards Brigade and were ordered to go to assist the 11th Indian Infantry Brigade, who were making slow progress in an attack on an Italian position at Bir el Gubi. Soon after we got there and when battalion commanders were summoned for an order group a strong mixed column of Germans appeared from the north-west. Unfortunately, we were the closest battalion to them so were immediately engaged with heavy shelling and Stuka dive-bombing. Bing Baylay was utterly fantastic, standing behind a shallow rise saying 'over to the right, slightly left, over the top' as if he was spotting for a shooting team at Bisley.

The enemy force didn't press their attack and seemed content to lob shells at us so we kept our heads down. The 4th Armoured Brigade appeared from the east and just before last light the Germans withdrew accompanied by the Italian Division, hastened by the RAF appearing and letting them have a thoroughly satisfying bombing and strafing attack, surpassing anything we had seen before. Having been under intense pressure to engage the enemy at all costs it really was a delight and a relief to see them get blitzed by our flyers.

It was around this time that news filtered through that the 21st Battalion of the 2nd New Zealand Division had captured General Johann 'Hans' von Ravenstein, the commander of the 21st Panzer regiment, and whose tanks we had seen blown apart by the RAF. The 21st Panzer division had lost most of its tanks in battle with an estimate that only about 25 remained in service. How we knew this bewilders me. Did we have a team in the desert counting destroyed tanks?

Following this spectacle, we met a number of small, isolated parties of Germans looking very bedraggled and unhappy whom we took prisoner. Taking a prisoner is quite a thing. Initially one feels a strong urge for retribution against these bastards who are responsible for the deaths of so many friends. However, that emotion is soon replaced by compassion as one sees the exhaustion of combat in their eyes, realising that they too have suffered from the turmoil of war. That said, there is quite a strong elation at capturing the enemy and knowing that however small a thing it is, this depletion of force might have an impact on some future engagement. There is another reaction to the capture of the enemy. When in battle, the advancing troops, tanks and vehicles appear amorphous, without any human element. Just a giant machine bearing down on you, hurling death and destruction. A prisoner brings a different perspective, someone not much different to us, if at all. Thrust into this catastrophe by the evil genius of Hitler and his cohorts and no doubt wondering at the futility of it all. Probably glad to be out of it and we helped with that by speeding them back behind our lines.

As we drove forward, we were on the south flank of the Germans and continuously harassing them, but their positions held out against us. The Germans also continued to exact a heavy toll in prisoners taken and vehicles knocked out.

On one occasion we were escorting a large supply of petrol up to tanks which had moved right up behind enemy lines and were hoping to attack as they retreated. Three 109s flew low overhead and started performing aerobatics just above us. They provided excellent target practice for our anti-aircraft gunners and one was hit, crash landing nearby with the other two scarpering. The pilot was furious, thinking his own troops had brought him down, and greatly surprised when he discovered otherwise.

Life was strenuous and very tiring. Breaking camp at first light and moving out into the desert. Engaging the enemy and getting shelled and attacked by aircraft, moving again at dusk and not settling down until late at night. We were living off hard rations and had little sleep. We certainly had no comforts. There was no observable front and no safe rear and we were not really sure what was going on. However, as December approached there was a feeling we were wearing the enemy down and their losses were mounting. Then came the breakthrough in early December when it was clear they were on the run and we heard that Tobruk had been relieved.

We temporarily transferred under the command of the 4th Armoured Brigade and undertook to try and cut off enemy forces but had little success. We advanced north towards Derna where we made life uncomfortable for any traffic on the road. I found this constant change of command annoying and at times quite depressing as it seemed we were groundless and were being moved hither and thither at whim. Almost as if no-one quite knew what to do with us.

We re-joined the Guards Brigade and were directed on points on the coastal road north of Agedabia. From the top of the escarpment at Sceledima we could see clearly that the enemy were retreating with flank guards well out to the east and we followed them hoping to cut off stragglers. The Axis army was still a considerable force and strong enough to discourage a rash pursuit and was quite likely to make counter-attacks. We were to the south of the main Support Group and the Axis forces clearly thought us a more serious threat, and very early one morning before we had broken camp attacked our column with tanks, forcing us to make a hasty withdrawal which we achieved just in time, with shells bursting around us and a number of vehicles and men being blown to pieces. I realised that something had happened to me. I no longer felt the deep sorrow at losing men and friends. It was as if my emotional juices had drained out of me leaving me devoid of tenderness. It was a relief really as it meant I was more capable of tolerating this constant destruction of life, but I wondered whether it meant that forevermore in my life I would have lost the ability to care.

In late December we transferred yet again under the command of the 22nd Armoured Brigade in the area of Hasseiat. We moved south expecting the enemy to continue its retreat but unexpectedly it established a defensive line south of Agedabia in soft sand country which made going very difficult. Soon enough we bumped into a major enemy force and the whole battalion was engaged in a massive firefight. While B Company came out of it without too much damage, A Company was engaged by a surprise column from the north and suffered very heavy losses, also losing their company commander and almost all their company headquarters. After an action such as this our focus was on getting the wounded away for medical attention and the dead had to be left where they fell. Only later would we be able to attend to their burial and by then it was not unusual to see scorpions coming out of the mouths of the dead and flies and ants feasting on their decaying flesh. This was the most horrible of things to deal with and deeply disturbing.

This action persuaded the enemy to move back to the Agheila area and we followed to establish a position in Mersa Brega, right where we had started out at the beginning of the year, making one wonder at the stupidity of it all. The German attack back in March had resulted in countless lives being lost yet had ended up accomplishing nothing, other than leaving the desert littered with burnt out tanks, vehicles and of course many thousands of bodies.

Now both sides were happily entrenched and not in the least inclined to do anything but regroup, we were able to enjoy Christmas Day without incident and had enough recently delivered supplies to give the men bacon, egg and sausages. What an enormous treat this was after surviving on bully for so many months!

Shortly after our Christmas festivities, I heard loud cheering start amongst the troops and rushed towards the noise, which was now being taken up by troops nearer to me. There was a staff car approaching which by all accounts contained Brigadier Jock Campbell and this gave us a terrific lift in morale. We had experienced so many situations where an anticipated victory was suddenly the exact reverse and we were withdrawing at speed, the arrival of Campbell gave us new hope as his reputation preceded him. He formed us into columns with the 2nd Royal Horse Artillery and the Northumberland Hussars and this gave me a chance to renew friendships made earlier in the year.

It came as a shock to learn that soon after Campbell left us he was killed in a driving accident; such are the perils of war. Here was a truly great commander, who had been at the forefront of the battle both strategically and physically, killed not by a shell or bullet, but by his driver taking a corner too fast.

We stayed at Mersa Brega until 19 January 1942, enduring the inevitable air attacks and undertaking patrols of the enemy positions. Near our HQ was a large Bedouin camp which flew white flags from their tents and at various strategic points. One evening at about 5 o'clock a formation of three squadrons of Italian C.R.42s and Stukas flew over, so I assumed we were in for yet another pasting. To our horror they started dive bombing the encampment and the screams from the women and children were terrible to hear. Hard to forget and even harder to forgive. This must have been a deliberate act of savagery against defenceless people caught in the unwelcome clutch of a war they had no part in.

On 19 January we were relieved by the 1st Battalion and wearily journeyed back about a hundred miles east to a well called Saunnu where we were expected to rest and recuperate for a week or so. However, in a complete reversal of what happened in April 1941 the Germans advanced just a day or so after we had left, and their advance was faster and more purposeful than a year before, and had we still been in position I have no doubt we would have suffered considerable losses.

We had been told that no movement was envisaged for some days, which the cynics took to mean that movement was probable very shortly, and how right they proved to be. Our Battalion liaison officer went off to report to the 2nd Armoured Brigade HQ and found them gone! We were placed under the command of the 1st Support Group but this only lasted a few hours before being placed under Vaughan-Hughes Force which was a composite force of the regiments resting in the Saunnu area. The next day we were in contact with the enemy and inflicted a fair amount of damage, but it was confusing as the enemy were driving both their own and British vehicles making it hard to decide what to shoot at. In the firefight we got separated from the other companies and continued to retreat towards Charruba, which lies some 30 miles south of Maraua, where after receiving an instruction to wait, we were reunited with Colonel Purdon.

At this point Rommel's Africa Corps had become overextended and could not continue its attack, so both sides dug in, allowing us a very welcome chance to rest and recuperate.

Chapter 5

A Well-Earned Rest then Back to the Front

After a couple of months guarding supply dumps, patrolling to the West, which attracted a good deal of attention from the Luftwaffe, we were sent to rest and refit at Buq Buq by the sea, some three months after our disturbed rest at Saunnu.

The Guards Brigade organization was magnificent; on arrival tents had already been set up, messes were established, and an unlimited supply of beer was laid on. Leave trains were organised from Matruh.

Here we were visited by our new Colonel-in-Chief, His Royal Highness the Duke of Gloucester, and soon after by the King of the Hellenes. I am sure we all thoroughly enjoyed turning out for these two! Buq Buq was not immune from Luftwaffe attacks but clearly orders had been issued by German High Command not to upset royalty. Buq Buq by the sea brings images to the mind of beach umbrellas and sun loungers, with much frolicking in the sea. It was pleasant enough, but the Luftwaffe had a habit of disturbing our peace from time to time.

After our three-week holiday we prepared to re-join the 7th Motor Brigade now under the command of Brigadier Callum Renton. The brigade consisted of us, the 2nd Battalion, the 60th Rifles and the 4th Royal Horse Artillery. It was intended that we would form an all-round defensive position capable of holding attacks by the enemy armoured forces while our own tanks manoeuvred to engage them. Having been attached to so many different commands it was a pleasure to be with the 2nd Battalion and the 60th. Later on we were joined by the 1st Battalion, fresh from leave in Cairo.

In May 1942 the tempo of things began to get quite feverish as it was clear the Germans were preparing for something big. The 9th was posted to midway between Acroma and Bir Hacheim to guard a field maintenance area, to the north the 1st Battalion was ready for immediate counter-attack, and in the south the 2nd Battalion was digging its defences.

Rommel was preparing to have another go at Tobruk and according to our intelligence reports planning to push forward deep into Egypt in an attempt at knocking us out of the war in this region.

On 25 May the Germans advanced with much more speed and direction than anticipated. While we were out of it at that time, we heard that the 2nd Battalion had been forced out of their defensive position and were in rapid retreat. Further north the Germans were heading for Tobruk and had little interest in diverting to fight localised battles, so we were out of range of the main battle. We did fire our ineffective 2 pounder guns at some German infantry, who were probably lost, managing to put some vehicles out of action and capturing a few prisoners but little else of note happened.

The main battle raged around a box position called 'Knightsbridge', which lay about twenty miles south-west of Tobruk, and the 1st Battalion was heavily engaged in all the thrusts and counter thrusts against the enemy. We in the meantime languished where we were until receiving orders to join the battle on 30 May. We firstly moved west with orders to relieve the French defending Bir Hacheim, accompanied by the 60th Battalion. Once in the vicinity we undertook a preliminary reconnaissance without incident but soon after there was a concentrated attack on it by Junkers 88 bombers which did not bode well. The next morning as preparations were being made to move into the town a sandstorm blew up and carried with it a strong force of German tanks, artillery and infantry which we were no match for. The French evacuated the town under cover of our artillery and after some intensive rearguard fighting, another dust storm hid our retreat. This second storm was a full blown khamseen which cut visibility to zero and caused most of our trucks and carriers to boil like kettles. We struggled on for long enough to be certain the Germans were nowhere near us then stopped to sit the storm out. As it died away, we had the task of cleaning sand out of engines, guns and equipment. The sand filled every part of our uniforms, had found its way into sealed food boxes, clogged our artillery and it felt as if it clogged every pore in our body. It was at times such as these that you wished more than ever to be out of this ghastly desert.

After getting our equipment cleaned and snatching a brief sleep over-night, we were ordered north to Bir el Gubi and from there we were drawn into the main battle around Knightsbridge and occupied a 'box' at Elvet el

Tamar on 8 June. This is where the 1st Battalion was fighting hard against Germans coming at them from all angles. The battalion was trying to prevent the Germans moving north and cutting off the 4th South African Garrison and the 50th Division.

During the day we would protect the armour and be subject to shelling and bombing. At night we would be expected to go out on patrol to gather intelligence on enemy dispositions. It was exhausting and there was no let up as the battle raged on and on. We were being worn down, losing armour and men at a fast rate and by 13 June were ordered out of the box position to retreat to Tobruk, in the company of the 1st Battalion. I was exhausted, filthy, stinking of cordite, desperately thirsty and just forcing myself to function. The men were in a similar state and looked to me and Bing to keep us from catastrophe. Collins was in his element. Seemingly endless energy, patience and courage. He knew when to shout and when to hug, keeping the men focused on the fight which was now more one of survival.

We were at the centre of the battle to prevent the Germans breaking through by Acroma to Tobruk. That evening the enemy tanks got right up to the 6-pounder battery positions where the two remaining guns were in action. Six tanks were hit before all the gun crew became casualties and leaving only one gun capable of firing. A senior fellow officer in the 1st Battalion took over and loaded and fired the gun single handed till his right arm was shot off.

On it went and we were ordered to move down an escarpment towards the coast road and then east to Tobruk. This proved very difficult as the tracks down were either mined or occupied by Germans. On the evening of the 14th June we did find a way down, but it took seven hours and we knew the Germans' tanks were approaching from behind us. Exhausted drivers fell asleep at the wheel causing others to crash into them. We just made it and by the time the enemy tanks formed up on the ridge we were out of range. Seven hours to move three miles!

After this retreat the exhausted battalion entered Tobruk and were ordered to prepare to act as a mobile reserve in the centre of the defences. The 1st Battalion went straight on further east to Gambut where they spent ten days out of the battle. After one day, and with much disgruntled muttering, we were ordered to move out of Tobruk east to Sidi Rezegh where we operated in columns for several days, again under constant bombardment from the enemy, then ordered further east to the south of Mersa Matruh. In the last days of June we were moving as quickly as possible towards the Alamein Line in close company with the Africa Corps! Our C Company excelled itself during our retreat. Paddy Boden recounted the tale later when things had quietened down and this is what he said. They had been ordered to try and defend the main road a few miles west of Dabaa in order to cover the evacuation of that place. It was felt that the town had already been evacuated but even so they set out in the middle of the night to occupy a position rather speculatively chosen from a map. They heard the sound of heavy machinery moving which on closer investigation confirmed that it was German trucks moving east. Boden decided to attempt to cut the road, thus separating this force from the advance force further on, even if only temporarily. He positioned his men behind small hills to be ready to shoot the moment it got light. His anti-tank guns and machine guns held centre stage protected on the flanks by motor platoons. On the given signal everyone let loose onto a completely surprised enemy with the result that sixteen vehicles were knocked out and a number of prisoners taken. This went on for three hours by which time the enemy had brought up enough fire power to dislodge the company, so they scarpered. It was greatly enjoyed both in the doing and the telling and did much to encourage our drinking to its success when things had stabilized.

Tobruk by this time had fallen making us feel a degree of relief that we had been ordered to withdraw, even though at the time suffering from extreme fatigue we were not at all happy. That aside we were withdrawing in utmost confusion with orders and counter-orders complicating matters and worst of all occasionally in the company of the enemy, neither side quite sure who the other was. Our withdrawal finally came to an end on the 2nd July and we had been in constant battle for over a month. We were exhausted, filthy, hungry and desolate at the disaster that had befallen the Army. Our Battalion had acquitted itself with distinction and had fought a great battle without flinching. There are many stories of valiant leadership, extraordinary courage, daring raids inflicting heavy damage on the enemy and utter determination not to succumb. We were defeated but still resilient.

We were to learn later of the catastrophe at Tobruk. We had been led to believe that the plan was to evacuate the city by sea but these plans had been countermanded with the result that 33,000 men and 1,400 tons of precious fuel were captured. It had fallen very suddenly after a breach by a Panzer division, through a perimeter weak spot.

When we finally stopped our rush East, we came together in the mess and Captain Mac McColl told us a greatly amusing story about the appalling state of our carriers, which by then had completed some two thousand miles and were in a terrible condition. We had been sharply attacked by tanks, and a herd of camels looked after by Bedouin Arabs had the same idea of withdrawing as we did. Mac said, 'I didn't mind much when the camels going fast shot past me; it really didn't worry me when a Bedouin galloped past us on a donkey – but I did begin to get a little anxious and think the carriers weren't much good when a Bedouin passed me on his own two feet.'

The Alamein Line was not a defensive line at all, just open desert with a large collection of people and armaments. What it did have in its favour was the navigable area was narrow with the Qattara Depression to the south and the sea to the north. The Qattara Depression was not a sea in itself but a sea of soft sand making it almost impassable. Defensive positions were being dug but not yet complete.

We had a few days rest and then were despatched to plug gaps in the defensive line, never staying in one place very long. It was depressing work coming under the command of regiments for brief periods and never feeling as if one belonged anywhere. We heard that the 1st Battalion was still fighting hard and claiming some success in terrible conditions of heat, dust and the stink of unburied bodies.

The Germans, having failed to break through in the north sent a major force south, but this was eventually stopped in its tracks and subsequently pounded hard by the RAF with much loss to the enemy. This battle, fought by the 1st, 2nd and 7th Battalions, as part of the 22nd Armoured Brigade and the 7th Motor Brigade, as well as Indian, New Zealand and Australian divisions, and probably many others, was decisive in preventing the Germans from threatening Cairo, giving the army vital time to repair the damage suffered and make preparations to break out of the Alamein Line. We were engaged in what was to become the First Battle of El Alamein, and the fighting both to the north and south of where we were was by all accounts some of the most vicious of this campaign. We were not called into this battle, nor were we threatened by it. We had to prepare to defend a new front should the Axis succeed in penetrating our lines either north or south.

At the end of July, the two armies stuttered to a halt, both physically exhausted and short of supplies. Rommel had tried every which way to break through and had failed. Until his lines were re-supplied he would not be able to press forward with further attacks. As it turned out this was as far as he would get and before the end of the year he was in retreat.

As July moved into an even hotter August, we settled into a much quieter routine with time to wash, eat and sleep. My fellow officers were able to regale us with stories of their great adventures, and at sadder moments we quietly reflected on the loss of good friends. We were never sure whether some had been killed or captured as it would usually take months to find out. In the heat of battle companies and platoons got separated. Surviving members would later reappear, bedraggled, thirsty, often wounded but with little knowledge of their fellows other than of those in close proximity. Other times we were told with great certainty that someone had been killed only for the corpse to reappear bearing a wide smile, having 'wandered' around the desert for a few days.

We had become a close-knit group of men who had learnt to rely totally on each other, learnt to make level-headed decisions under severe duress, learnt to lead with compassion and fortitude, and above all to keep fighting, even when it seemed as if the gates of hell were open and welcoming.

As a result of this fellowship we assumed that we would continue to operate as the 9th Battalion Rifle Brigade, a member of the 7th Motor Brigade and part of the 8th Army. However, this was not to be. We heard that our battalion was to be disbanded and the men either assimilated into other battalions or returned to the UK. After almost two years of intense hardship and sacrifice we were to be chucked away like an empty can of bully. There were openings in the other battalions, but I felt at a loss at what to do as deep down I hungered for something different. It was tempting to return to the UK and see what was on offer there but at the same time I felt the battle here in the desert was approaching its climax and it would be good to see it through, having vested so much into it so far.

As it happened the decision was almost made for me. I was contacted by an old friend who had left the Battalion to join David Stirling's Special Air Service and he suggested that I might like to come and meet David for a chat. He said that David remembered me from the time, so long ago now, when we were together in Chamonix. David was forming a new squadron and he was very keen on officers and men from the Brigade as they had complementary skills to what was needed for the SAS. Before I was able to travel to meet Stirling we had the little matter of winding up the Battalion to deal with.

Purdon invited all the officers of the 9th to Cairo for a celebration of its time in North Africa and a farewell party which General Jumbo Wilson attended. After so many months of hardship it was a very welcome relief and we made full use of the gin on offer with the party extending several days in various parts of Cairo! What I found amusing was having Squeak Purdon and Jumbo Wilson hosting our party.

After this revelry I travelled to Kabrit and met with David Stirling and a Major Mark Kerr to discuss joining the SAS and this went well as almost immediately I was offered a tentative position in B Squadron, which was the newly formed squadron expanding the SAS by about 60 men. I took some leave in Cairo then returned to the Battalion to assist in its disbandment and say farewell to men I had fought with over the last twenty months. Quite a few from the Brigade were joining the SAS so I was going to be in good company. Riflemen Handscombe and Levy would eventually form part of my section after our training. I was not surprised that so many were attracted to the SAS, and for the SAS we were excellent candidates. We had operated deep into the desert and at times in constant engagement with the enemy. We had learnt to travel in the desert at night and find our way without any light other than what we got from the sky. We had become experts in stealth, almost as if we were wraiths of the night. We were tough, battle hardened, had lost good men, seen horrific wounds and learnt that within us we had the strength and resilience to keep going under extreme duress. We knew also that it was a lottery who lived, who got maimed and who died. We were all of us men prepared to put everything on the line and those that died just got unlucky. I remember standing on an escarpment watching a tank battle below and the chap next to me stopped talking mid-sentence. The bullet could just as easily have hit me.

What motivated us to press our luck is beyond me. Maybe we had become addicted to danger and the intense excitement of close contact with an enemy intent on killing you. Whatever it was, the lure of the SAS was strong so that is the way a number of us went.

My final farewells were to Bing and Mike Collins. Major Bing Baylay had been the best commander I had ever served under. He had managed to keep up the morale of B Company with his unruffled temperament, humour, patience and unbelievable decision-making ability in the face of terrible stress. Bombs falling from Stukas, shells exploding nearby fired by tanks not so far away, bullets zinging off vehicles, trucks exploding, men screaming in agony and others slumping to the ground dead, and there was Bing relaxed and focused, issuing orders and taking little care to protect himself. He was quite exceptional, and I felt great sorrow leaving his company.

And then Collins. Everything said about Bing one could say about Collins. A Company Sergeant Major of great character and strength. His eyes were everywhere, and his organizational ability was exceptional when endeavouring to sort out the mayhem of close engagement. His actions on many occasions saved us from being overrun by the enemy and the men worshipped him. He was absolutely critical to our survival as a Company, with a seemingly inexhaustible energy and never once did I hear him complain or talk of his own needs. I looked him in the eye, shook his hand, wished him well and will never forget him. He had my respect and I knew I had his.

During our time in North Africa the Rifle Brigade had suffered more than 60 officers and 400 men killed in action and many hundreds more captured or injured. We also lost officers and men at sea while being transported to or from this theatre of war, the most widely known being the *Laconia* sunk in September 1942. The Brigade had earned itself a place at the top table in the North African campaign displaying extraordinary feats of courage and tenacity, often with lamentable armour against far superior German weaponry. The bravery of its commanders and men was nothing other than extraordinary and the preparedness to sacrifice life and limb for their country humbling.

In a despatch from Cairo in August 1942, the war correspondent Godfrey Talbot explained what the 7th Motor Brigade had spent its time doing in the following despatch to the BBC, and my father had kept it for me to read when I finally got home in 1944. I found it surprisingly touching and it really did manage to capture the spirit of all that we had done over the period from January 1941 to August 1942 and what the other battalions had achieved earlier so I have decided to reproduce it here.

'Some light can be shed on this sort of desert warfare by telling a little of the story of the 7th Motor Brigade; experts in the art of harassing the enemy, appearing from nowhere behind his lines, and creating swift destruction amongst supplies and transport. Some of the exploits of these men have been described from time to time and there have been awards for gallantry which have brought out scraps of the story; but the 7th Motor Brigade's recent history is little known. These men who operate like Bedouins in the desert, are mostly Londoners, which a patrol officer once described as a "regular No.11 bus load". A good 30 per cent of them are regulars who have served in India and Palestine. The Brigade includes battalions of the Rifle Brigade, the King's Royal Rifle Corps (KRRC) with Royal Horse Artillery, Royal Army Service Corps, Royal Engineers, Royal Army Medical Corps and light Ack-Ack Battery. In the old days, the 11th Hussars and latterly King's Dragoon Guards and South African Armoured Corps joined.

'The Brigade has, in strength varying with its job, 6-pounder anti-tank guns, 25-pounder field guns, Bren carriers and, when needed, armoured cars and tanks. The Rifle Brigade and the KRRC components are, of course, motorised infantry and are the core of the Brigade. In desert fighting, this motor brigade has done things which are acknowledged as military classics. Take the rear-guard action on the 8th Army's southern flank, from El Gobi to the Alamein Line. The men of the Brigade worried and delayed the enemy: they never lost their mobility, and their petrol and ammunition supplies had to be brought anything from twenty to sixty miles west of the enemy's most easterly point of advance, and yet the supplies reached the column every night.

'The Brigade, or most of it, used to be part of the Seventh Support Group; they were a part of it when the Italians first crossed the Egyptian frontier two years ago. The famous Group was commanded by the late Lieutenant General Gott – Brigadier Gott he was then. Since then they have been up and down the desert from Alamein to El Agheila; they've come to know the country almost as well as their own Battersea, Hammersmith

Broadway, and other places in London to which many of them will not return but where their tradition will stand very high.

'When Rommel's attack started in May this year, they were making themselves a considerable nuisance to the enemy south and west of Bir Hakheim. They fought successful delaying actions, they destroyed lorries and tanks, they upset lines of communication. And later, behind the enemy's line again, they took many prisoners: they recaptured 100 of our own men and shot down an aircraft. They protected the withdrawal of the Fighting French from Bir Hakheim. Here and there they held the enemy for precious days in the hostile blue again – somewhere there – probing and darting in to strike at the enemy's southern flank. They don't get much sleep; they don't get much rest, but nor do the enemy's supply columns when such raiders are about.'

I have recently finished reading Hastings' book of the Rifle Brigade from 1939 to 1945 and noted his summing up of the life of the 9th Battalion in the desert war from late 1940 to August 1942, when it was disbanded as was the 60th Rifles. This decision was taken due to the calculation that it would be impossible to maintain the strength of four battalions.

He writes, 'The 9th Battalion was seldom lucky in the desert. They arrived as part of a division which was split in half shortly after their arrival. Subsequently the Battalion never remained under the same command for long at a stretch: at twenty-four hours' notice or less they would be switched to another brigade or division. Their longest stretch – and a happy one – was with the Guards Brigade, and when they finally left their command the Brigadier Marriott wrote Colonel Squeak Purdon a charming letter in appreciation of their services in the brigade.' In total they were under the command of twenty different Brigades, Groups or Divisions, and on a time elapse, twenty-seven.

He goes on to say, 'The Battalion was for long periods in contact with the enemy. It visited every well-known place in the desert from Alamein to Agheila. The fact that it was continually changing command did not make it any easier for the Riflemen, who were engaged like anyone else in night patrolling, in escorting guns, in being bombed and shelled, in evading enemy tanks, in contracting desert sores and going short of water, in brewing tea in twenty minutes and cooking bully in twenty ways and in navigating across miles of desert.'

Later in the book Hastings comments on the disbanding of the Battalion: 'After the farewell party in Cairo attended by General Jumbo Wilson, to all intents and purposes the Battalion ceased to exist. It is sometimes difficult to understand the complex working of the Higher Command. Presumably they were happy at this critical moment in the fortunes of the Eighth Army to dispense with the services of an experienced battalion, proved and tried in eighteen months of desert fighting.'

Chapter 6

A New Life with the SAS

After the pounding I had received over the last year and a half and the emotional consequences of experiencing the destruction of so many young lives, it even surprised me a little that I was still capable of taking the fight to the enemy. I was still alive when so many of my fellow men were either dead or brutally injured. There was an anger in me that burned intensely and drove me on. An anger at the tragedy of this war and the sheer awfulness of what the Germans and Italians had inflicted on us. I could still hear the screams of men burning to death inside a tank, the cries of mortally wounded men in the heat of battle without the means to help them as we were at the time fighting for our own lives. And the constant threat of death from the air, especially in the first year. The scream of the Stuka arrowing down, the release of its bomb and the concussion of the explosion. Later on, when the RAF got its act together the immense pleasure of seeing these purveyors of death being shot out of the sky. And the stories of the SAS attacking airfields deep within enemy territory destroying many planes on the ground reducing the enemy's ability to fight in the air.

I felt calm and determined. The SAS was a natural step for me and many others in the Brigade as much of what it did was what we had been doing already.

In September I journeyed to Kabrit and after a few days we started training under Mark Kerr. There was a mixed collection of individuals from other regiments, some old hands from the desert and some looking for a quick path to glory. The latter lot didn't last long. Mark left after a few weeks for the Yorkshire Dragoons and was replaced by Major Vivien Street, who joined from GHQ in Cairo. Pat Hore-Ruthven and Philip Morris-Keating had each been troop commanders in the Brigade as I had so I felt in good company. Pat became a close companion during those days of assessment.

He had recently been a company commander in the 1st Battalion and had fought in the battle of Alam Halfa which I had been fortunate to miss. Pat was five years older than me and had joined the army after Cambridge, serving in Malta and Palestine before being moved to Cairo at the outbreak of war. He shared my passion for fox hunting, and we had both raced in Point to Point. He was married to Pamela Cooper, a well know society figure at the time, and had two young children.

Those of us who completed training in early November 1942 were told that we should prepare for an operation deep into enemy territory leaving around 20 November. Vivien had pushed us very hard to root out the hangers on and as a result a good number of recruits had not made it through. I felt in very good shape after the gruelling two months of hard and challenging assessment, confident that I would do whatever was demanded of me. The time away from contact with the enemy was also therapeutic. The men were tough and independently minded, with as much influence as the officers over who remained and who was chucked out, resulting in a quite different relationship to what I had become used to in the Rifle Brigade. This is not to say that the men there weren't from the same mould, but the formality of command was more rigid. Our training had included a course in parachuting, lessons in bomb use, desert navigation, endurance training and the laying of mines, much of which we were already expert in. We were fit, mentally tough and ready to head out to wherever our eccentric and charismatic leader directed.

The training and assessment had taken place in and around Kabrit in Egypt, which was a major RAF station and where the SAS had been formed in 1941. Kabrit lies about twenty miles north of Suez and eighty miles east of Cairo. It is a desolate area devoid of contact with any social life and the occasional trip into Cairo for a couple of days leave had been welcome although we always seemed to end up in a bar fight so maybe we were best kept isolated. We had been keeping track of a great battle being fought at El Alamein during the latter part of October and early November and the exhilarating news of the 8th Army success in driving Rommel's army back into Libya, having inflicted considerable damage. There was still much hard fighting being done and Rommel was by no means giving up.

As we pared down the numbers to the eventual sixty men that would make up our squadron I reflected on the skills and character needed to become part of this disparate regiment. Almost exclusively the ones that succeeded getting selected were quiet, self-effacing men with a burning determination to succeed. The ones that left us tended to be more brash and arrogant, more inclined to revel in the status that would be garnered by becoming part of it. Most importantly it was strength of spirit rather than physical strength that differentiated. The urge to succeed, even when exhausted and to never give in unless death is the only alternative. We also needed to be able to work as a member of a small team recognising the strengths inherent in each of us. Given the type of work we were expected to do we had to have absolute confidence in the ability of our fellow men and we had to look out for each other at all times. Because the selection process was so demanding we had confidence in this latter point as the only ones who got through were of this calibre.

Early morning on 18 November Vivien Street called his officers to his field tent for a briefing on the foreshadowed operation. There were going to be a lot of us travelling nearly two thousand miles across sometimes very difficult terrain to reach our operational area running from Bouerat to Misrata in Libya. He explained that the Eighth Army had reached Agheila, south of Benghazi, and we would push through their line in a few days' time. There was a coast road running the length of Libya used by both German and Italian transporters bringing troops, munitions, fuel and provisions from Tripoli to supply Rommel's army to the east. Our job was going to be to disrupt road traffic in preparation for the next push forward by the 8th Army. The initial attacks were all to take place at the same time and afterwards each troop would attack as opportunity arose. We would meet with A Squadron run by Paddy Maine when deep in the desert a few days into the mission.

My section consisted of three jeeps and five men. I had asked for Handscombe and Levy to join my troop and they were as delighted as me to find we were together again. Each jeep carried two men, although some had three, two Vickers K machine guns, a rifle, a sten gun, pistol, seventy-two gallons of petrol, twelve gallons of water and twenty days of rations. In addition, there were two thousand rounds of ammunition, a hundred pounds of explosives, a case of ten mines and some money to be used to bribe the Arabs. In total there were thirty jeeps and fifteen three-tonne lorries to carry additional supplies.

I listened carefully to what Vivien was saying as it seemed we would be so far behind enemy lines without easily accessible supplies that our chance of getting out was remote. I raised this and was told that it was expected that the Eighth Army would make its push forward in December thus bringing them much closer to our position. I had a feeling that this was a sop as the speed of advance in a battle depended to a large extent on the behaviour of the opposition and it was slightly far-fetched to believe that the Germans were going to roll over. True, Rommel had received a good pasting at El Alamein and was licking his wounds, but he had a history of turning an apparently dire situation around and he would not give ground away easily. That said, this was what this operation was all about, disrupting supplies to make it more difficult for Rommel to do anything other than retreat west. I still had my doubts and reckoned our chances of getting back were slim. I had signed up to this regiment knowing full well that it took extraordinary risks and lost many lives doing so and there was little point challenging orders.

I spent the next couple of days with my men loading the jeeps, checking that everything worked as it should and double checking that we had all our equipment, especially spares for the jeeps. I made sure that the men had packed warm clothing as the desert can get very cold at night. I was excited about the mission and found I was in good company as the men were itching to go. We all ate as much as we could lay our hands on knowing that the coming weeks were going to be spartan. This excursion into the unknown in the company of such excellent men was incredibly exciting and so different from the previous two years. It was without doubt a great adventure, akin to taking on one of the great mountains of the world. We were going to drive deep into German and Italian held territory and create mayhem with only the slimmest of chances of getting back in one piece, if at all.

Zero hour came just before midnight on 20 November accompanied by frantic last-minute checks that we had everything we should before the long convoy of vehicles left the base and thundered down the road towards Cairo to our west. The night air was balmy with a hint of moisture and it was refreshingly cool sitting in the jeep gazing up at the brilliance of the desert stars above. Our long convoy made good time to the outskirts of Cairo which we intended to bypass as best we could to the south.

We journeyed on into the depth of the night with the jeep kicking up over ruts in the road jarring my back as we bounced up and down on the hard seats. All I could see was a plume of fine sand ahead of me as our fleet of vehicles was causing quite a sandstorm. It filled every crevice in the jeep and blanketed our coats, sneaking its way beneath our clothes. We rested up in a wadi the next morning for several hours then off again into the early evening light until we reached our way point between Bardia and Tobruk, after a journey of 500 miles. We had made good time, with the whole convoy arriving safely, albeit in need of some repair. The site was ideal with an oasis garlanded with palm trees offering welcome shade from the fearsome sun. We brewed up food and large mugs of tea, replenished our water, and slept for the rest of the day.

On the evening of 24 November, we moved on by road towards Tobruk, bringing with it memories of the raging battles we had had a year before. This road had been cleared by the 8th Army, so we were able to make good progress with little to fear from the enemy. After resting up near to Tobruk our long convoy made its way further west until reaching At Ain El Gazala, about twenty miles west of Tobruk, where we were joined by David Stirling and Carol Mather who had journeyed directly from Cairo.

We then drove along the coast road past my old favourite Benghazi and Agedabia and south of El Agheila before turning south and venturing deep into the desert. Driving through this area brought back memories of our battles there and the losses we had suffered. It made me feel surprised that I was still alive and still functioning. The area was littered with burnt out tanks and mangled field guns. The journey of some two hundred miles was tough with the three-tonne trucks frequently getting stuck in the soft sand and needing to be dug out, an exhausting process especially as they would invariably get stuck again soon after. However, we made good time and met with A Squadron in the region of Bir Zalten pretty much as planned. A Squadron was about the same size as ours so there was a mass of vehicles and men milling around.

A Squadron had been there for a few days and had prepared the camp well with caves hollowed out of the chalk and sandstone cliffs to provide sleeping quarters and cover for the vehicles. Fires were burning and we were welcomed by the delightful smell of food being prepared. Everyone appeared to be busy checking engines, cleaning weapons, and working on the jeeps.

We crashed out for a short while before being called to a briefing by Stirling and here I met Paddy Maine for the first time. He was charming, friendly and relaxed, and gave the air of a man completely at one with the war. His reputation as a ferocious fighter without fear for his own safety was well known to all of us.

David was filled to the brim with energy and with a recklessness that while enervating also suggested the welfare of his men was not a priority when it came to attacking the enemy in his own back yard. As our briefing progressed it became more apparent that our squadron was the expendable one, given the depth of our incursion into enemy territory. Still we had a job to do and I listened intently to what he was saying.

A Squadron was made up of more seasoned men and was going to operate further east than our area giving them a better chance of making it back to the British Line, which should be advancing towards them. Their operational area started almost due north of where we were at a place called Agheila then running west for about 200 miles to a town called Bouerat. This would become the most easterly area for our sector. Our operational area was going to be another two-hundred-mile stretch of coastal road running from Bouerat to Tripoli. This meant we had another five hundred miles to travel just to reach the eastern end of our sector and a further two hundred miles for those operating near Tripoli. Paddy's operation would start as soon as he was able to move his squadron into position and he would be ahead of us by at least a week.

Our task was to disrupt the enemy supply line at night by blowing trees over the road, planting mines, and when possible shooting up soft skinned vehicles. The objective was to make night movement so unbearable it would force traffic to move by day leaving it vulnerable to attack by the RAF. It would also act as a tourniquet on the delivery of vital supplies needed to sustain Rommel's army against the planned attack by the 8th Army at the same time. The broad plan to disrupt traffic along a four hundred mile road was an ambitious one and if we could keep it going for a couple of weeks it would have a real impact on the outcome of the forthcoming battle. David told us that he had received a communiqué from his commander Colonel Shan Hackett saying that Montgomery felt our activities could have a decisive effect on the course of the battle.

Each raiding party was to operate every third night for as long as possible starting on 13 December and not later than 10 January as at this time it was predicted that the 8th Army would relieve us. I thought it highly unlikely that there was any chance that we would survive that long, not least because of access to supplies and fuel. The execution of the plan was to be left to individual commanders with each section consisting of an officer and five men in three jeeps. Our areas of operation were given as follows:

> Captain Galloway, West of Tripoli
> Captain Maloney, East of Tripoli
> Captain Mather, Khoms
> Me, Khoms-Leptis Magna
> Two Free French, Leptis-Misrata
> Major Street, Misrata
> Captain Hore-Ruthven, South of Misrata
> Captains Alston and Thesiger West of Bouerat.
> Captain Oldfield to rove between A and B Squadrons.

Philip Morris-Keating 150 miles from the coast on the road running south to Bu Ngem.

David would lead our squadron and he intended to roam about taking whatever opportunity arose to disrupt the Italians.

Carol Mather, who was to operate in the area adjacent to mine, had arrived at the rendezvous with David Stirling and this was the first time we had met since our meeting in Chamonix in early 1940. He was lively, acutely intelligent and great fun to be around, with amusing stories of the operations he had been on with the SAS. He had joined the regiment in June of this year and had seen a good deal of action in the few months before our coming together. Montgomery had asked him to be his ADC but although he started in this role David had persuaded him to undertake one last mission with the SAS and he expressed grave doubts that we would make it back. Whenever we had the chance, Carol, Pat and I would chat about life before the war, and with both of them gregarious and filled to the brim with wonderfully amusing stories our laughter would bring a smile to even the most dour lips, although thankfully there weren't many of those in the squadron.

We had three days here to repair vehicles, clean kit and plan the trip. We were in a location with good cover and there were no enemy aircraft around to spot us. We all needed to rest and feed well to better prepare ourselves for the ordeal ahead. This was my first operation with the regiment, and I was beginning to get used to the lack of structure and the almost freelance feel of day to day living. We were being sent into combat with a flamboyant disregard for our survival coupled with an expectation that we would be able to find a way through. That we might not seemed an irritating distraction. David had a habit of waving things away when pressed, muttering implausible platitudes and wandering off. I guess that once we had been delivered safely to our operational area, he would roam around moving quite rapidly towards A Squadron.

After a few days of sorting ourselves out we parted company with A Squadron and set off on our long journey towards Tripoli keeping well away from the coast as we were now in enemy territory. We battled on night and day, only sleeping between dawn and about 10am, catching up rest when possible by dozing in the jeep as it careened across the hard, rocky sand. The nights were bitterly cold, and we needed all our layers on to retain a semblance of warmth, but the days were warm enough. We constantly scanned the sky for fear of being spotted by an enemy plane and would be very exposed should one make an attack.

We were effectively sitting on top of a bomb, so much ordnance was packed into the jeep. The desert proved to be extremely difficult, rough, hilly and in some places soft sand country, and the three tonners got bogged down all too frequently. However, driving in the cold of the desert at night under the brilliance of the Milky Way and the glare of an over-bright moon was exhilarating, even though the fine sand being thrown up by the lead jeeps found its way into every cranny. We drove night and day for five long days, stopping just long enough to sleep and eat. Sleep was always in short supply as we pushed on with such haste. The going was incredibly tough, and it took much longer than planned and was to result in a decision made later on that almost proved fatal to our mission.

We got to our second base, east of Wadi Talmar, early in the morning of 2 December, and after brewing up a good breakfast I was at last able to lay up under our well camouflaged jeep and sleep the sleep of the dead, right through the remainder of the day, oblivious to the flies buzzing around my face. I awoke greatly refreshed, aching with hunger as the cool of the desert evening descended on us.

It was here that we had planned to leave the three tonners with supplies of food, fuel and ammunition. It was a good spot with excellent cover from the air and we were confident that it would remain secure. We had lost one of the trucks on the way and had managed to transfer most of the supplies across to the remainder.

Most unfortunately, we were spotted by a small Italian aircraft which circled us for a while before disappearing over the horizon. We swiftly scattered the vehicles over a wider area and camouflaged them as best we could and as anticipated some bombers appeared escorted by three fighters. Fortunately they were not able to spot us and after flying around for an hour or so they gave up. However, we were now on the map so the enemy would be on the alert making our task all that more difficult.

After this excitement I chatted with Mike Sadler who had built quite a reputation as a top-class navigator and who always travelled with David, leading endless raids against the enemy. He was from Rhodesia and had built his skills with the Long Range Desert Group before being picked out by David when the SAS was formed in 1941. He was friendly, if taciturn, and seemed at ease with his extraordinary life. He told me of times when, having completed a raid and exhausted from it, David would suggest something else and off they would go, guns blazing into the night, planes exploding, fuel dumps lighting the desert sky and terrified enemy soldiers running hither and thither completely bemused by the ungodly drama unfolding around them.

We left this haven after a day or so and the journey became extremely difficult as we descended into Wadi Talmar which had been deemed impassable by the LRDG. This was the decision I spoke about earlier and it nearly wrecked our chances of getting to the road. After entering the Wadi at night, we had to stop and lay up due to the damage done to a number of our jeeps. The chief problem was broken half-shafts and the crown wheel in the differential breaking. So many jeeps had been damaged that David ordered us to cannibalise parts from two of the jeeps under the command of Captain Galloway and bring along the third as a working spare. He was to be left with some rations and his men to make their way back to the trucks.

Having done our best with repairs, we pushed on into the Wadi and spent the next four days driving over a tortuous route of rock-strewn ground and soft sand. We were plagued with punctures and damage to the jeeps and progress was interminably slow. Eventually we broke out having built a track up its steep side – to my knowledge, the first time such a route had been taken. It did not bode well for us if we ever needed to make an emergency run back to the temporary base.

For the next day or so we drove towards our objective of Misrata, on the coast of Libya about ninety miles east of Tripoli. We were dog tired and in desperate need of a day's rest, but David kept up the tempo insisting we push on with all speed. The men were uncomplaining, although I was aware that, should we see action, we were not going to be able to work things out as quickly as we might hope to. My body felt sluggish and my mind was as if it were steeped in porridge, not a good condition in which to approach the enemy.

Chapter 7

Into battle

On 10 December and late in the afternoon we approached a major road that ran from Sirte to Misrata and found ourselves in immediate danger of being spotted as there were Italian posts all over the place. It was here that David decided to leave Philip Morris-Keating and his troop with orders to lie up in the sandhills and take whatever opportunity that presented itself to inflict damage to enemy traffic.

Time was getting tight and we had to push on to the oasis of Fascia in order to meet our objective. We hid behind a ridge and took a long look through binoculars but couldn't see any life in the posts so assumed they were not manned, and it was worth pushing forward to cross the road. We were anxious not to be seen because a group of our size would alert the garrisons posted along the road to our presence and make our operation almost impossible to accomplish.

David signalled that we should move forward, and all twenty jeeps revved engines and moved quite fast from behind the ridge into open desert. As this long phalanx of soldiers in jeeps moved towards the road, I heard the sound of heavy machine gun bullets ripping into the side of the lead jeeps, the first of which was driven by Pat Hore-Ruthven. His jeep was knocked out but Pat leapt onto the bonnet of the one behind and they drove onto the flank of the two armoured cars attacking us, engaging them with the Vickers, which was enough to distract them from the main body of jeeps which swept across the road and into broken country beyond, where there was decent cover. While the bullets of the Vickers could not penetrate the armoured cars the noise inside would have been deafening and enough to terrorise the Italian crew, who may well have believed there was greater danger to come.

Unfortunately, at the start of the engagement, one of the jeeps blew apart in the melee resulting in two men being killed and all ordnance and provisions being lost. Two crews were left in the area to bury the dead men once the danger from the armoured cars had receded and they re-joined us a few hours later.

We were lucky heavy cloud brought a rainstorm which prevented any attempt to attack us from the air, but we knew we had to press on as fast as possible to get clear of the area.

We set off to our final RV which lay in a deep and scrubby wadi near the oasis of Bir Fascia offering good concealment. Here we would dump surplus provisions we had carried to be used to replenish what we would carry into battle. We reached this at midday on 11 December having rested for a few hours before dawn. David gave us our final briefing before casting us into the wilderness of an uncertain future. He said that if we ran short of supplies, we should return to the dump at Fascia and this would be replenished should the Eighth Army not reach Bouerat in the next ten days. Montgomery's attack was to begin the following night and was expected to reach as far as Misrata. David then said he had been called back by Hackett to headquarters at Kabrit so would now leave us but not before he had a little adventure of his own with Mike Sadler and off he went towards the road to the north. As time passed it had become more and more obvious that our squadron was expendable and there was little chance we would get out as the supply lines were just too long and the chance of surviving in enemy territory until the 8th Army arrived remote.

The 'Bir' or well, was an underground cistern made by the Romans, and it held a large quantity of water. We were therefore able to top up our depleted supply, have a delightful shower under a jury-rigged water tank and eat our last decent meal for a while. We were behind schedule so there wasn't any time to have a decent rest.

We had travelled 1,900 miles over rugged and at times almost impassable terrain, suffered endless stops to repair tyres and damaged half-shafts, foraged for water to replenish dwindling stocks and had lost several jeeps and a number of men. That said, we were all set to go and after we had rested, the sections began to drift away towards their operational areas. Carol was my immediate neighbour, so we set out together in our six jeeps across increasingly and rather concerningly cultivated ground that impeded our progress and brought into stark relief the difficulty we were going to have keeping concealed. Our whole modus operandi was hit and run, from one concealed position to another. If we were surrounded by Arabs this was going to be very difficult!

The Italians had got very twitchy over the past months after stories of many such raids had circulated – jeeps bounding out of the desert night with Vickers guns blazing tracer into their midst, trucks blowing apart, planes exploding with loud crumps and fuel dumps igniting lighting the sky for miles around. Their next experience was going to be the sudden terror of a truck running over a mine, forcing it to slew off the road, spilling its cargo of people and supplies and burning itself out. We planned to drive into the resultant mayhem causing even more panic and this was partly the point of the mission. It wasn't just to cut supply lines but to weaken resolve also. Fear breeds cowardice and many thousands of Italians had surrendered earlier in the campaign in North Africa while enjoying overwhelming superiority. We were not there to capture prisoners but make it more likely that the opposition would cut and run or surrender when up against the main force.

As we got close to our respective operational areas, Carol and I said our goodbyes, wishing each other well and wondering whether we would ever meet again. My area was the road running from the west of Khoms to the east of Leptis, about fifteen miles in total. Khoms was a substantial town with an Italian garrison and Leptis an ancient city with extensive Roman remains. It was a busy area and we were going to be hard pressed to remain concealed. It had rained heavily during the past two days making going very difficult and soaking us in the process

My fear of struggling to find good layup spots was well founded. When we got to within six miles of the road, finding good cover proved difficult and we ended up under patchy scrub with our camouflage netting draped over the vehicles. A gnarled shepherd ushering a herd of goats wandered by, rapping a stick against low acacia trees to chivvy them forward and looking at us with apprehension and curiosity. He asked if we were Italian, which I denied vigorously as I knew they were not much liked, and I tried to pretend that we were Germans, but I wasn't sure he bought into this ruse.

On 16 December and in the deep of the night we moved north and blew a couple of trees onto the road to block it before withdrawing to a low ridge lying about a quarter mile to the south. After several hours of lying in the cold no trucks had come along from either direction so I joked with the men that both Captain Mather and the Free French were clearly doing a very good job! We withdrew about thirty miles south of the road and laid up under better cover in a shallow wadi with good recesses to escape the sun and nose the jeeps into. We were left undisturbed by Arabs and were fairly confident by now that the shepherds we had seen the day before had not reported our presence. The problem now was our petrol was almost exhausted and we only had enough to get back to the road one more time and hope to be able to syphon fuel off a damaged truck.

On the night of 19 December we journeyed north and had better luck. We had laid a couple of mines on the road and a large supply truck was hurled into the air with the force of the massive explosion. It then rolled onto its side, decanting its load and burning furiously. The driver and passenger were killed in the explosion. We saw the truck behind it screech to a halt with the driver desperately trying to engage reverse gear. We drove out from our ridge and as we got to within fifty yards let rip with the Vickers and within seconds it blew apart with a mighty bang suggesting it was carrying explosives of some kind.

Anxiously I noted that behind the truck there were a number of troop-carrying vehicles that had swerved off the road and were heading towards us at speed. We turned tail hoping to escape into the darkness of the desert, but the going was too slow over difficult terrain and the Italians were in hot pursuit. I cursed as the cloud broke open allowing a bright moon to partially illuminate the desert with its eerie, colourless, ghostly light. After a half-hour I signalled the jeeps to turn and face the enemy in the hope of slowing down their advance. When the lead Italian vehicles got to about 300 yards we let them have a prolonged burst of fire using the Vickers guns on all three jeeps, the tracer reaching across the dark desert, with some hitting metal and shooting spectacularly up at an angle and into the night sky. Without waiting to see the effect this had we turned south and drove as fast as possible in the hope of finding cover.

One of the jeeps ran out of fuel so after hastily grabbing the rifle, sten gun, ammunition and water, the two men jumped into the other two and off we went again. In the gloom we couldn't see any sign of the Italians, so our delaying tactic had worked. Both jeeps were now stuttering from lack of fuel and it was a miracle we came across an accessible wadi. With open desert around us and no fuel we had to pray that the Italians would not find us, giving us a chance to get away on foot once the chase died down.

It wasn't long before we heard the sound of engines approaching the wadi and more moving behind us. With the jeeps now well camouflaged we pressed ourselves against the side of the wadi. After a while listening to the fast gabble of nervous Italians conversing just within earshot, I heard the sound of men approaching along the floor of the wadi to our left, and sure enough several Italian soldiers moved cautiously towards us, still unaware we were there. It wasn't until they got very close to us that we were spotted, and we had no option other than shoot them down, as they hastily raised their rifles to do the same to us. This action alerted the Italians to our presence although not our position. We waited until they were very close before using concentrated fire to push them back. Every time the Italians probed forwards, we would fire into them and then move position so that they couldn't get a fix on us from muzzle flashes. I was still hopeful the darkness would eventually work in our favour and give us a chance to get away, especially if I could persuade the Italians moving behind us to engage the Italians to our front, creating enough chaos and mayhem to allow us to slip away.

We tried firing in both directions at the same time, then ducking and running further along the wadi, but the Italians weren't falling for this ruse. I sent two of the men out to see if there were gaps in the Italian lines, but they reported that we were all but surrounded. This game of cat and mouse went on for another half-hour or so before the ammunition started to run out. As the eastern sky began to lighten with the approach of dawn, I tried a last-ditch diversion to allow the others to escape, should this distraction be successful in creating a small gap in the Italian positions.

Crouched low I ran down the wadi and crawled up its shallow side where there was a small boulder offering some protection. This brought me onto the flank of the Italians, who were about 100 yards away, and all firing with great enthusiasm.

I was carrying one of the rifles and opened up with this and it seemed to do the job as much of their attention was drawn to me. I kept my head down as my position was torn apart with a torrent of incoming fire. I slid back down the wadi and moved a further twenty yards and engaged them again. The net was closing, though with shots coming at me from both sides of the wadi my ammunition was rapidly depleting. With little hope of escape I put my head down and ran as best I could further down the wadi but within a couple of minutes saw a large body of men approaching me. I skidded to a halt and raised my hands, hoping there was now enough light to let them see I had surrendered.

I knew I could not expect a smiling welcome after inflicting so much damage and there was a good chance I would be shot. The Italian soldiers appeared confused that I was on my own, clearly expecting a much larger force. A captain led the troops towards me and the look on his face did nothing to make me feel that this wasn't my last day. When he got to me, he grabbed the rifle from the trooper next to him, stabbed it hard into my midriff and pulled the trigger. It was a moment of exquisite silence following the noise of battle over the previous three hours. To me it seemed as if all things stopped at that moment and time was stretched and extended, with the faces surrounding me stilled in the early morning light. And then a switch was flicked and reality returned.

The captain stared at me with an expression of disbelief on his face. It seemed to defuse the moment and he backed away, allowing the barrel of the rifle to drop before handing it back to the trooper. I noticed his hands were trembling and his face was so tense his skin was drawn back. I felt strangely ethereal, exhausted by the battle, and somehow removed from what was happening. An enormous sensation of relief coursed through my body and I suddenly found myself out of breath. The captain issued orders to his troops to move further down the wadi in search of other men and assigned three of them to take me away.

I was marched roughly out of the wadi and over the hard stone-strewn sand to a couple of troop trucks and, with evil looking bayonets encouraging me on, climbed aboard into captivity. This was a dire moment for me, and I began to feel utterly dejected. All the excitement, the disappointment, the proximity to death, the loss of good friends and the men under my command and the constant toil of war, and now captured. Questions buzzed around in my head: Should I have found a way out? Was the quest doomed from the start? Had our mission made the slightest difference to the AXIS war effort? What had happened to the other sections, especially Carol in the area next door to us. Had my men managed to get away? My mind was whirling.

I was driven to Misrata and ushered into a large building with endless corridors. We turned down one and came to a low door which was opened with a large ornate key by the guard. Beyond it was a dismal room with a few low wooden beds with no-one else in it.

I lowered myself onto one of the beds and lay back exhausted, feeling drained of all emotion after the tumultuous last month. I hoped that Carol Mather, Pat Hore-Ruthven and Vivien Street had enjoyed better luck than me with at least part success of the operation, although I knew it was unlikely given how far behind enemy lines we were. It was 21 December 1942, I was a prisoner subject to the whim and possible brutality of my captors, and I was utterly crestfallen. I reflected on my decisions during the time we had been operational near the coast road and whether I could have avoided capture and managed to escape. At the time I didn't know that almost all the sections had been either killed or captured, which would have given some balance to my thoughts. I felt I had failed my men and the squadron, and the blame rested firmly on my shoulders.

Later that morning I was joined in my cell by a rakish chap who said he was an RAF gunner shot down and crash landing a few days earlier. At first I was tempted to chat with him about the raid as I felt a strong need to justify my decisions, which were weighing heavily on me. Something held me back though as I had an instinctive doubt about him which I couldn't quite put my finger on. He appeared to be acting disconsolate rather than really being so and I felt the trauma of being shot out of the sky would weigh more heavily on him. I questioned him closely about his squadron and where it was based, what planes he flew in and number of crew, and after a short while smelled a rat. He tried to turn the conversation to me with a number of questions about how I was captured and my regiment, all of which I parried. I began to cruelly mock him to see if I could break his story and he looked more and more uncomfortable. I then told him I was going to have a sleep, and in the meantime, he might like to bugger off; and bugger off he did.

After just a day or so in the cell, eating only disgusting watery soup with a couple of wedges of bread, I was loaded onto a truck and driven to Tripoli, about ninety miles west of Misrata. I sat at the back of the truck with the flap open, an Italian guard on my left and one opposite, both with machine guns clasped casually. The journey gave me a chance to look out and I noticed that there were check points and patrols on bridges and corners, some even on straight roads, and that trucks were bristling with guns both front and rear. It was some consolation that, while the mission had not been a success, it had at least put a considerable wind up the Italians. I noticed also that there was a fair amount of traffic on the road in the middle of the day, which gave the RAF a chance of strafing, which was a key objective of the mission.

The truck headed straight to a wharf in the port of Tripoli and I was bundled across a gang plank onto an Italian submarine. I was ushered down the forward hatch into a smelly, dimly lit steel corridor leading to a cramped forward torpedo storage compartment. To my dismay there sat a forlorn Carol Mather. I slumped down beside him and we shared our tales of the last few days, both having experienced much the same problems. He and his team had been spotted driving through a village at night and were discovered by Italians while laying up the following day. They escaped on foot but were hounded by a large number of overexcited Italians, accompanied by ever increasing numbers of Arabs. While they still had ammunition and with good sharpshooting, they were able to keep their pursuers at bay. Inevitably though they were surrounded and, out of ammunition, had to give themselves up.

There were about fifteen officers in this claustrophobic compartment with its fetid air. It appeared that I was the last one to come aboard as almost immediately I felt the submarine get underway. From the downward motion I guessed we were submerging, and this was soon confirmed as the rolling motion ceased. Later on, there was quite a lot of noise and commotion in the boat followed by the thuds of depth charges exploding nearby, which went on for half an hour or so leaving us all very nervous at being trapped in this metal tomb. It is quite a terrifying experience being a couple of hundred feet below the surface when at any moment life can be crushed out of you. There was nothing we could do other than sit gripping knees trying not to panic as the deep thuds reverberated off the hull. I had thought I had become inured to fear but this was the most dreadful experience imaginable and I could visualise the consequences very well. The odour of real fear permeated the compartment, so I knew I was in good company. After things quietened down tight smiles were shared and we talked with surprising frankness about how we felt, which helped a great deal to release the tension.

We crept along for four days without much food and little contact with any of the crew. This is where we spent Christmas Day 1942, cooped up in a tiny enclosure with a couple of torpedoes for company and a slop bucket stinking in the corner. We had to sleep on a hard metal floor breathing foul air and without being allowed out to exercise. We could feel the roll of the submarine from time to time so assumed it had surfaced at night to recharge its batteries. After four ghastly days of confinement we were taken out singly to the conning tower to breath fresh air and I was able to see Sicily to the north of us, the towering peak of Mount Etna dominating its eastern end. The indescribable bliss of breathing cool fresh air and to feel the wind on one's face.

Chapter 8

Italy and confinement

We eventually docked against a low wharf in the port of Taranto, which sits snugly inside the heel of Italy and were immediately offloaded. Escorted by several armed guards we were marched into a waiting truck, there to take us to the railway station for a journey up the eastern coast to Bari, and a transit PoW camp. We arrived at the camp in foul weather with torrential, cold rain falling onto cheaply built wooden huts surrounded by a tall barbed-wire fence with ominous looking watchtowers dotted around the perimeter.

The other inmates in our hut were huddled around the only stove and made no effort to find space for us. We were fed near starvation rations of soup and a bread roll with the probable aim of making us weak and less likely to attempt to escape. Carol and I discussed possible routes out, one of which was to use a pair of coffins made up for the emaciated Yugoslav prisoners dying off in numbers in an adjoining compound. About 800 of these poor people had arrived in the camp in early January. This idea eventually came to nothing but at least gave us something to focus on. Towards the end of February our plan had to be abandoned when with little notice we were moved out of Bari onto a train north that was to take us to Chieti, lying a few miles south of Pescara. We plotted again on the train with an ambitious plan to escape during a night stop at a station but unfortunately were kept in a siding until dawn under the watchful scrutiny of two guards, so the escape plan foundered again.

The large camp at Chieti was reached later that day. Campo 21 was laid out either side of a wide thoroughfare that ran directly from the main gate, through a barbed wire and wooden second gate to the end of the compound and its fifteen-foot wall.

There were around 1,300 officers and other ranks, most of whom had been there for a while after the fall of Tobruk. Of these there were about 100

Americans, mostly pilots. It was a cramped, cold miserable place with only just enough food to keep us alive. The camp had been rife with jaundice and dysentery, with filthy conditions and an intermittent water supply. Our bunk beds were crammed together and as a result life was stressful. Fights would break out over the smallest of things and resentments would fester for days.

Occasionally Red Cross parcels were received. These helped supplement our poor diet and also contained precious tobacco. I felt fortunate to have arrived in early spring at a time the weather was warming as inmates complained about the harshness of winter and bitter cold. Also, within a month or so of our arrival Red Cross parcels started to be more liberally distributed which I gathered had been held back by the prison commander, Colonel Massi, and his thoroughly unpleasant sidekick Captain Mario Croce. These two were becoming more amenable as a result of Mussolini losing his grip on power and the likelihood of Italy breaking away from the Axis.

Carol had decided that he had a better chance of escape if he was in a camp nearer the Swiss border and quite ingeniously swapped identity with another prisoner who was due to be transferred to PG49 at Fontanellato, in the Plain of Lombardy. He paraded with the new draft and the disguise appeared to work well enough for he was marched off into the waiting trucks. It was a sad moment when he left the camp as he had become a good friend over the preceding four months.

I slowly adjusted to camp life, with all the difficulty that occurred from having far too many men crammed into a space designed for 400. Discipline was maintained and much effort was made to keep our spirits up with lectures on various subjects, a good theatre group and the all-important escape committee which was overseeing various tunnel projects. Our senior officer, Lieutenant Colonel Marshall, was affable and appeared to be a good mediator between prisoners and the camp guards, although later on he would infuriate me and many others in the camp with his passivity.

Initially I had found capture and incarceration a relief. Even though conditions in the camp were squalid it was peaceful compared to the constant stress of combat. By the time I was captured in December 1942 I had been either preparing for, resting from or engaged in action for two years. During this time, I carried responsibility for my platoon and my company, I had had to lead patrols into enemy held territory, both night and day, and sleep anywhere time allowed. I had somehow escaped injury even as those around me had fallen, but it began to dawn on me that some injuries can be hidden and less easy to cope with. If you have a bullet in the arm it is a job for the surgeon and the nurses. If you have the devil in your head, it is the job of the psychoanalyst and there weren't any in our camp. There were plenty of men deeply traumatised, disappearing for days into their personal corridor of anguish, with a pervading attitude in the camp that we just had to get on with it.

When in the field of conflict there is little time to think about these things but here in Chieti there was too much time and the nightmares came. Nightmares of horrible intensity, visions of things so awful as to be the stuff of the nine circles of hell in Dante's Inferno. My nightmares were very much in the seventh. I found myself questioning decisions I had taken in the heat of battle and whether they resulted in the loss of life of men who trusted me and depended on me. I know it was silly as most of the time we were under so much immediate pressure it was a battle for survival, and we carried ourselves well. But my men were my responsibility and losing them, at times to horrific death, was deeply scarring. I needed a good friend to talk to, and soon after Carol left I found one.

He was Peter Gunn, a lieutenant in the Rifle Brigade who had been captured in 1941. I found him to be a congenial, pleasant and erudite man with a strong desire to escape. He was four years older than me and while he was born in Sydney, Australia, he had spent most of his upbringing in the UK. We formed a good friendship over the next few months, giving me an inkling that if I was going to make a break for it, he would be a dependable companion. He was a good listener without the urge to provide answers and seemed to have a deep understanding of the turmoil in my brain. His personal experience of war wasn't that much different to mine although he had enjoyed the success of fighting the Italians in 1940 and hadn't experienced the ferocity of the Africa Corps. He had been captured on a night patrol while crawling alongside the enemy line assessing gun dispositions and minefields. He encouraged me to talk openly without flinching and after a while I felt myself begin to mend. I had been brought up in a Victorian atmosphere at home where emotions were parked in a dark corner and much was the same at school. This was the first time I had really opened my mind and heart to someone, and it brought great relief. He opened my eyes to the fact that most of the officers in the camp carried with them the consequence of battle and that there was nothing at all to be ashamed of. He allowed me to realise how courageous I had been, leading from the front, remaining focused and clear-headed in the frenzy of battle which in all probability saved more lives than it lost. I had never thought of my own bravery up to this point, and acknowledging it was like applying a soothing balm to a tortured skin. It allowed me to reflect on the valour of the men under my command and acknowledge that it wasn't my fault they had died or suffered grave injury. I had friends in my life, some of them very good friends, but this friendship with Peter was quite different. He was someone I could share confidences in a way that was entirely new to me. I had complete trust in him, and I will always remember him for the depth of his understanding and the wisdom of his counsel.

During this time my energy returned, and I focused more on finding a way to escape. I am a tall man and tunnelling wasn't my first choice, nor was anyone very interested in giving me that opportunity as the groups were well established. Peter and I discussed a number of ambitious plans to get out, but none bore fruit.

Conditions in the camp improved marginally when about 300 of the prisoners were moved out in early summer, and the Italians, mindful of what might happen if Italy accepted terms from the Allies, became more willing to further increase the distribution of Red Cross parcels. It was around this time that news filtered through that Rommel had been vanquished in North Africa by the combined force of the 8th Army and the Allied 1st Army. This was a marvelous moment for me, learning that the toil, bloodshed and loss had resulted in a major and possibly defining defeat of the Axis armies. It was a glorious moment and the camp came alive with celebration.

With the warmth of the summer sun on our backs we kept ourselves fit with games of football and American softball and on occasions were allowed to walk outside the compound walls. At times we were even allowed to travel away from the camp and swim in a river although a better description would be to paddle. The joy of this was we were able to wash in the cold water and we would return to the camp happy and stimulated. We heard news of the Allies invasion of Sicily and the 8th Army's progress through Italy and our spirits were raised at the prospect of freedom.

We struggled to be patient while waiting for our chance and it came in early September 1943 when the Italian government surrendered to the Allies and ordered all Germans out of Italy. While the Germans didn't take a blind bit of notice of this ineffectual order it did take them time to reinforce areas vacated by the Italian army, giving everyone in the camp the chance to get out and make their way south, towards the approaching 8th Army.

In this relative chaos, Marshall, in his wisdom, was sticking to an order from the British that PoWs should not attempt to escape the camps but remain and await the arrival of the Army. This seemed utterly ridiculous as the upheaval was the best chance of escape so far, especially for those who already had a plan, such as the tunnelling groups. Marshall was adamant and even put British patrols on the perimeter of the camp with an order that any man found attempting to escape would be court martialled for desertion! What seemed certain to us was the 8th would not reach the camp before the Germans did, so staying, as ordered by Marshall, would lead to an extension of life as a PoW. Allied planes were seen flying close by the camp which gave me the idea that if I could escape, waiting for the 8th to arrive would be a better option than trying to find my way south with the increased risk of recapture. Peter and I started to make plans, and as they advanced, excitement between us increased. The long boring days began to shorten as we filled all available time with ideas for the future. We were greatly tempted to disobey orders and walk out of the camp one evening, as did a number of others we chatted to. Word of this must have filtered up the line of command as we were all brought before Marshall and told that as serving officers in the Army our duty was to obey orders from a senior officer and any deviation from this would result in severe disciplinary action being taken. It would be rude of me to write my thoughts of the man as we left the parade ground.

Chapter 9

Escape!

I awoke from a fitful sleep in the small cave high in the Majella mountains to find snow had fallen overnight, quite heavily it seemed. Some of it had blown into the cave and the wind picked up the flakes to swirl around my face and blanket. It was bitterly cold and I knew that I had only a little time left before I would be too exhausted and famished to make the journey across the remaining ridges, which I had to cross in order to reach the Allied line.

P eter lit a cigar. Its acrid smoke vaguely masked the foul odour filling the cramped water tower in the camp grounds, where four of us needed to remain concealed as the first step in our escape bid. On 20 September 1943 we had exercised our plan to evade capture by the Germans now occupying the camp and were installed high in the tower with a good view of the camp below.

Over the past few months Peter and I had become as close as brothers. His natural sense of the ridiculous kept me amused and his sardonic treatment of the Italian guards was delightfully funny. He had learnt basic Italian, and this was to prove most useful during our escape. The other two in the tower with us were Captain MacDermott of the Royal Engineers and Lieutenant Rickett of the Royal Northamptonshire Regiment, known as Mac and Ricky. I knew them less well but the four of us were united in our determination to escape rather than succumb to imprisonment by the Germans and the certainty of being moved into a PoW camp in occupied territory north of Italy. A couple of weeks before, I had noticed the door into the tower was ajar and took the opportunity to explore. There was a ladder rising vertically against a brick wall leading through a wooden floor and on up to a small hatch providing access to the water tank. Closing the door, I climbed the twenty feet or so up to the first level which measured about 15ft by 15ft and contained bits and pieces used to service the tank. The dusty floor was made up of loosely fitting planks with gaps wide enough to see the access area below, and there were two narrow windows side by side open to the elements. It was big enough for up to four of us to hide and I thought an ideal place if the chance came to avoid being transferred away from the camp by the Germans. The risk was that someone might want to climb the ladder to the water tank if it needed attention. I talked it through with Peter and the next day we wandered casually through the camp, without attracting any interest from the other men milling around kicking pebbles with hands in pockets. To our intense frustration we found the door locked. Peter suggested we chat to one of the other ranks who had boasted about being a locksmith before the war and whom Peter thought was more likely to have been a safe cracker.

We kept the tower under observation and noticed that twice a day an Italian worker would come to turn the water on and an hour or so later turn it off. He would wander off to have a smoke and chat with his mates, leaving the door open and the key in the lock. We took our now friendly lock expert along with us and with Peter and I standing chatting and shielding his body he made an imprint of the key. I have no idea how he managed it but a few days later he presented us with a key and to our delight it worked. He was well rewarded with our ration of cigarettes and some additional food.

We started to make plans and Peter introduced me to Mac and Ricky who had got wind of our proposed escape and suggested they join us. They were pleasant enough company and we felt having an engineer amongst us might have its uses. They had already collected a supply of food and had acquired helpful information about where we might head once we were free of the camp. At this time security within the camp was non-existent, other than the British patrols organised by Marshall, and this allowed us to make contact with the newly formed Resistance.

Early one morning a small group of German officers was seen in the Italian section of the camp and a week later a further visit was noted. Late at night on 20 September German trucks arrived carrying well-armed troops and this was our moment to act. We left our huts under cover of darkness and scurried to the tower carrying with us our carefully accumulated provisions. We were not able to lock ourselves into the tower as for some inexplicable reason the key would not work on that side of the door, something we hadn't bothered to check. We hoisted our supply of food, water and a slop bucket up onto the mid-level floor. There was a fair amount of room amongst the detritus and spares strewn over the floor. It was overly warm and we were to later discover inhabited by a large family of mosquitos.

The fact that there were so many prisoners left in the camp when the Germans arrived still seemed to me insane. What an extraordinary loss of opportunity for a large number of prisoners to escape.

According to Marshall, British command was trying to avoid having 75,000 PoWs roaming around the region getting shot or starving to death. While this was to some extent understandable there were about sixty in our camp who had dug tunnels and were therefore ready to go. There had been a window of opportunity lasting about a week, but permission was never given. Had we been allowed to leave during that time we would have been on our way south now and out of the hands of the Germans.

Given the number of German troops passing by the camp, they were going to resist the progress of the 8th Army in Italy rather than let the country go. One of my concerns, shared with the other three, was that an obvious line of defence was to use the Abruzzo mountains as a backdrop, to make any flanking move very difficult. If this was to be their plan it would bring the defensive line very close to where Peter and I had decided to hunker down. The question of whether to head south immediately or await the army was batted back and forth. On reflection the decision that Mac and Ricky took was the better one but at the time it was not so clear. Later I learnt that while a number of escapees did manage to get through the Allied lines that year, many others did not, some being recaptured, and others being killed.

The other PoWs without our determination and mostly those who had become institutionalised had been sceptical that we would get out and pessimistically said we would probably be shot if discovered.

We couldn't see or hear much as the risk of showing our faces at the window was too great but assumed that the first thing the Germans would do would be to take a roll call, and if they had information from the Italians about who should be on that roll it could trigger a search of the camp.

We hoped that they would assume that anyone not on the roll would have already made their escape.

With so many Germans now patrolling the camp it was imperative that we only spoke in whispers and under no circumstance knock over anything. Peter had brought a chest infection with him and it was particularly difficult for him to suppress the urge to cough. The heat was intense through the day and we poured sweat. When the sun dropped behind the Abruzzo mountains to the west, the air slowly began to cool, bringing welcomed relief. We had rations packed into a loose bag and enough water to see us through several days, so we tucked into our evening meal of cold meats and now stale bread, washed down with water. It was now the mosquitos decided to attack, greedy for our blood and relentless in its pursuit.

Early morning on the second day there was the scrape of a key being turned in the lock, which would have surprised the bearer as the door was not locked. Through a narrow crack in the floor we could see an Italian walk in and turn on the water for the camp. Two Germans stood just outside the door with guns slung casually across their shoulders, chatting and smoking cigarettes. Surprisingly he then left, locking the door behind him, so it seemed the Germans had asked for the water to be left on, which suggested to us that the prisoners would be moved out within a day or so and had been offered the chance to clean themselves before leaving.

After the excitement of avoiding discovery we settled down to the boredom and discomfort of the dusty, hot room, unable to chat due to the proximity of the German sentries. We sat propped against the brick wall, saying little and holding onto our determination to get out. We hoped that the locked door was not going to present a problem as it looked to be well made.

We fell into a stupor, knocked into a semi-comatose state by the uncomfortable heat. The smell from the shit bucket was overpowering and there was no means of escape from it. There was no movement in the fetid air, but our collective commitment to escape made this modest inconvenience worth enduring, so long as the Germans got a move on with emptying the camp. If they delayed this for a week or so we would struggle to continue.

Good fortune was at hand, for us at least, as trucks began to ferry prisoners from the camp on 23 September and this went on through the

24th with the camp falling silent on the 25th. The next morning brought the sound of children playing near the tower and when Mac poked his head out of the window to have a look he was spotted by them. Our cover blown we had no choice other than get out of the tower and take our chances. We climbed down the ladder to the ground floor but then had the task of getting out as the door had been locked and our key would not work from the inside. The door was a stout one and didn't yield easily to our efforts to break out and we eventually had to smash our way through it using pieces of servicing equipment that had lain strewn on the floor above. This clearly made a considerable amount of noise and had the Germans been anywhere nearby that would have been that.

Mac and Ricky remained determined to make a break south immediately and have a go at getting through, but Peter and I continued to weigh the odds and were still not sure this was the best plan, given the numbers of Germans we had seen moving past Chieti. We were desperate not to get caught and finally concluded that hiding out for a couple of weeks was a better strategy.

With the cool of the evening air wafting over us, bringing joyous relief from the discomfort we had suffered for the last three days, we moved cautiously away from the tower keeping close to the high wall on our left. The guard towers were unoccupied, which gave us hope, and there were no lights visible in any of the buildings. The fact that children had got into the camp was encouraging.

We had to move away from the deep shadow of the wall in order to get to the first gate that used to separate the prisoners from the guards, and which was our way out of the camp. This was the most dangerous part of the plan as we would be clearly visible if anyone remained in the guardhouse. To our huge relief, there was no guttural call of 'Halte!', no sound of a bullet being slid into the chamber. The area was empty and the wooden first gate was open. We moved cautiously through it and onwards towards the main gate of the camp which was partially open. Still no guards in sight so through it we went and at last were free of this place. What a wonderful feeling it was to have avoided discovery and find ourselves outside the camp.

During the days between the surrender of the Italians and the arrival of the Germans our escape committee had been able to establish contact with the Italian Resistance, prepared to help escapees, and we had a house to head to just 200 yards from the camp. We got there without incident and an elderly couple ushered us swiftly into the house and into a small damp room with a tatty rug on the stone floor and a few blankets piled in a corner. They spoke no English, so they indicated with gestures and nods that we should stay in the room and keep quiet.

Mac and Ricky came to shake my hand and set off on their great adventure. It was tempting to go with them rather than wait but Peter advised caution saying that it was most likely that that escape route would result in capture or death. Reluctantly I waved them away and they quickly disappeared behind some houses, heading east of Chieti towards the Adriatic coast. Again I pondered our decision to remain locally and wondered whether we had made the right choice. It all depended on how quickly the 8th Army pushed on and where the Germans established their defensive line, if indeed this was their plan. From the scant news we had to date, the 8th was coming up at speed with little opposition.

After a miserable supper we unrolled the blankets and lay down on the hard floor to sleep, only to find that this smelly little room was also plagued with mosquitos. After an uncomfortable night swatting and sleeping intermittently, the next morning brought pure joy as we were able to look out at the uplifting sight of the mighty Grand Sasso standing guard over the Abruzzo. The sun was already bright in the sky and the early morning late-September mist hung like a shroud over its lower reaches. It was a jewel of a day, almost as if it had been sent to welcome our release from captivity, and the two of us smiled as we stretched our limbs and breathed deeply the wonderful scent of freedom. We had a huge challenge ahead of us and our fate was uncertain, but for now we felt the exhilaration of being in charge of our future.

The Italians who had met us the night before gave us fresh under-garments so that we could bin our foul camp clothing, but we rejected the offer of fresh outer clothes preferring to remain in uniform. We were also given buckets of water to wash from.

Chieti was on top of a hill to the south of us and by all accounts was now occupied by a German battalion which sent out regular patrols and was of significant danger to us.

A chap purporting to be a member of the Resistance arrived during the morning to discuss moving us that evening to a house further into the countryside. We remained indoors through the rest of the day, and with dusk falling, our escorts arrived. Bidding farewell to the elderly couple we skirted the camp's southern side and headed south-west for some two hours, which took us about five miles from Chieti, in rolling countryside with good undergrowth for cover.

We arrived at a small stone house tucked discreetly behind some trees and accessed via a narrow track and were shown into a tiny damp room. We heard that the Germans had started rounding up Italian men and were conducting house searches. While our house was well screened, our Italian friends advised that we move further south-west towards the hill town of Pretoro, on the edge of the Majella Mountains, where there was little regard for the Germans and the fascists. They said they would organise this, but that it would take a few days. We spent three days at the house, quietly awaiting the guide who would take us deeper into the mountains. In the evenings we were able to stretch our legs and walk for an hour or so through the woods and small fields surrounding the house. The hills rose into mountains to our west and the occasional deep rumble of thunder could be heard as dark, menacing clouds shrouded the peaks. The early part of the day was gloriously sunny and it wasn't until mid-afternoon that cloud began to build bringing with it the threat of rain.

Early evening on 30 September a small party arrived led by a woman we were introduced to as Frieda. It seemed an odd name for an Italian but the others in the small party seemed to defer to her and she spoke good English which was a great help. We set off, and just after we started out we heard a deep pulse coming from the south followed by a sight so exhilarating it caused every nerve ending in my body to erupt with a glorious sensation. There, flying low over our heads, were three Spitfires, pulled along by their massively powerful and unmistakable sounding Merlin engines. Goose bumps covered my body and it was difficult to choke back the tears of emotion as both Peter and I realised that the Allies were closer than we thought. I hoped the sight of these planes swooping low over Chieti caused the Germans a moment's thought about their precarious future. We turned away to continue our journey, ebullient and in very good spirits.

As we walked, I chatted with Frieda who told me she had been born in the North of Italy, near Turin, and had married a man called Marco whom she met at university in Rome. His work as a civil engineer had taken them to the east coast of Italy to the town of Pescara. At the outbreak of war he was conscripted into the Italian Army, even though he hated the fascists and wanted nothing to do with the alliance with Germany. He was killed in North Africa in 1941 leaving her with a deep hatred of Mussolini and his government.

After Mussolini's arrest in Rome in early September he had been whisked away to a secret location but news had spread locally that he was being held at the Imperatore Hotel, on a plateau halfway up the Gran Sasso mountain, very close to where we were that day. He had been watched over by 200 well-armed carabinieri and the position was deemed to be very difficult to attack. However, on 12 September German SS airborne troops in ten gliders landed on the plateau and without a shot being fired secured his release.

Frieda felt the cowardice of the carabinieri was deeply shameful to all Italians and she burned with anger as she spoke, often slipping into Italian and losing me with the speed of her invective.

When she had got that off her chest and calmed down she spoke of the fledgling resistance groups that were forming this side of the Abruzzo and helped by partisans who had been fighting Italian Fascists since the outbreak of war. They hadn't yet undertaken attacks on the Germans and were quite wary of this, given the news from the west of Italy that German reprisals were savage, killing ten Italian civilians for every German killed. They were focusing presently on helping escapees to either find their way south or find a place to lay up.

I asked her about travelling south and she said she had little news of those that had gone that way but from the modest amount that had filtered back quite a few had been recaptured. She surmised that those trying to get through the lines would still be en route and she would probably never hear if they were successful. She asked me about my war and with a degree of trepidation I told her about my time in North Africa fighting against the German and Italian armies. She took this in her stride and appeared to attribute no hostile feelings against me. She was an erudite woman with an incisive grasp of politics and life in general. She was charming and attractive, and I found myself beginning to respond to her energy and charisma. As we walked into the evening sun we chatted about life before the war and how we pictured life when it was all over. I was very taken by her and even today can remember her wide smile, her iridescent eyes, and her long shapely legs tucked into leather boots laced up to her knees.

After covering several miles, she called a halt. I propped my back against a tree, sipping water from a shared tin water bottle while Frieda rummaged in her pack, producing cheese, figs and bread. Feeling replenished I lay down on the damp ground to sleep fitfully in the cold for a few hours until the sun slowly brightened the sky to the east and we had enough light to see the way through difficult but charming countryside.

The hills got steeper and the streams more rapid. We climbed higher and came to a small village called Roccamontepiano, which we skirted, climbing above it to a convent standing on a natural terrace with magnificent views east over rolling tree-clad hills to the coast. Here we rested and ate a lunch of bread and cheese, washed down with water from a nearby spring, cold and delightfully refreshing.

Frieda told us that there was little chance of being spotted as the Germans had not occupied this area. As we ate our lunch enjoying the warmth of the sun, four armed Italians appeared from the wood behind the convent and stayed a while chatting with Frieda before moving away towards the small village lying below us. Frieda explained that they had escorted four other escapees to Pretoro, the village we were headed to.

Sitting here being warmed by the autumnal sun and replete from my sandwich lunch I began to feel quite sleepy, but Frieda signalled that we should move on towards Pretoro as she wanted to get there before dark and the way was hard going with many steep hills to cross. The valleys were lush with summer growth, the deciduous trees still full of leaf and we were able to pluck figs from the trees as we walked. Our journey south along a ridge behind Roccamontepiano took us through mixed woods abundant with wildlife and after a few hours we dropped into a shallow valley before climbing towards the hill village of Pretoro perched above us, seemingly glued to the side of a steep hill.

Chapter 10

Pretoro

We entered the village at dusk and moved rapidly up steps rising through narrow alleyways formed by the high walls of houses on either side, eventually reaching a stone house on a small piazza near the church. Frieda took care to avoid us being spotted by any of the villagers because she said some were Fascist and informers. Using a heavy-looking iron door knocker, she rapped firmly a few times on the solid wooden door, then looked with some concern around the piazza to make sure we were not spotted. The door was opened by a deeply tanned, middle-aged man of medium height who ushered us into the house and with a final look at the piazza, closed the door and bolted it. Frieda introduced us to Gino Francioni, who she said would provide shelter in his home and then arrange accommodation elsewhere. She clearly knew Gino well and they chatted for a while but at a speed which rendered their conversation unintelligible to me. Frieda then turned to us and with her charming wide smile wished us well and for a safe journey home. She held my eyes and said she hoped that our paths might cross again someday. She gave Gino a final hug then opened the door and disappeared into the night. We were never to see her again and I often wondered what became of her in her fight against the Germans. How brave she was.

Gino had a resourcefulness and inner strength that we found very reassuring. He was the sort of chap you would like on your shoulder in a tight spot. No friend of the Fascists, who he believed had destroyed the whole fabric of Italy, he was committed to doing all he could to root out any in the village who might collaborate with the Germans. He brought worrying news that the Germans were likely to establish a defensive line close to Pretoro which would make life very difficult for the people and no doubt bring more Germans into the village. Presently there was only a small garrison in the lower village. In the meantime, we were advised to remain in the house, keep away from windows overlooking the piazza, and speak English softly. We were all too aware that his life depended on our not being discovered.

With that sombre thought in mind, we were ushered upstairs to a room looking out over the valley and where there was little chance of being spotted. It was pleasant enough, with two single beds resting up against the rough stone wall. Downstairs on the ground floor there was a bucket of water for washing, as well as a small kitchen and an area to sit and eat. He called us down and we enjoyed a supper of fried pieces of beef and pasta accompanied by a heavy red local wine that tasted wonderful after so many months of having little else to drink other than water. The room was lit by a couple of oil lamps and there were candles to light the bedroom upstairs. It appeared there was no electricity in the village and no piped water.

After dining he showed us down some well-concealed rough steps hewn out of the rock into a cellar which had an ancient wooden door leading onto a narrow alley behind the house and this, he told us, was how we would escape should the Germans come banging on the main door. Turning right onto the alley would take us to the edge of the village and a track leading away into the valley. He also pointed to a bed of straw lying at the back of the cellar and said this is where we would deal with our ablutions. In the bedroom there was a china pot for night-time relief. He said that he would descend into the valley each day to bring fresh water to the house and that we would not be allowed to roam free during the day.

After our adventures over the last week we were exhausted, and it was a welcome relief to collapse into a comfortable bed. Peter blew the candle out and we reminisced for a while on how fortunate we had been to make it this far and how freedom tasted so sweet. Peter slipped into sleep leaving me drowsily awake listening to the wind rustling through the trees in the valley and the cool mountain air wafting into the room. With a feeling of gentle satisfaction and a smile on my lips, sleep gathered me into its soft embrace.

I awoke to sun streaming through the small window and the sounds of a village coming to life. I felt greatly refreshed and very hungry. I went down to find Peter and Gino chatting at the kitchen table where there was coffee and bread, with figs and an apple. Gino spoke good English and had lived in the village all his life. He talked of the village and its history, the millers who ground flour in the cave mills in the valley, of the reputation the villagers had of being wood craftsmen and the harshness of life through the winter. With that he reminded us to stay indoors and away from windows and left for the day.

We stayed with Gino for three nights before he told us we had to move to the house of Titino and Maria Santurbano, tucked away in one of the many narrow streets rising steeply up the hillside. These cobbled streets offered many nooks and crannies in which to hide in an emergency. They were not lit at night, allowing us to get exercise and relief from the boredom of staying indoors all day.

The maze of streets offered a number of escape options and once we had marked out various routes, we knew that, with luck, we could get to the edge of the village and disappear into the valley where it would be very difficult for the Germans to track us due to the density of the forest.

Once it got dark Gino escorted us to the Santurbano house which lay up a narrow alley framed by tall buildings on either side. He rapped on the door and it was immediately opened by Maria, who was a stout woman with a welcoming demeanour. She had a niece staying with her called Juliana, a gorgeous 18-year-old who sparkled with humour. She was taller than average, had long slender legs and large seductive eyes. I was very attracted to her and we spent much time flirting, with me trying desperately to improve my Italian and she English. She made better progress than me as learning languages had always been an obstacle for me, although my father spoke fluent German and French, having spent time in each country before the first world war.

Peter was greatly amused by my limited vocabulary, and while I was beginning to speak reasonably well, I got completely lost when the family went full steam ahead. He made much faster progress than me and his Italian became quite proficient, something that was to be of great help to him when in a really tricky situation later on. While flirting was tolerated in Maria's household, it was made clear that anything more would result in either one of us being marched down the road to be delivered to the Germans!

Having welcomed us into her home and shown us our comfortable room, Maria asked us to join the family for dinner. We sat in the kitchen eating a wonderful meal of chicken casserole washed down with good amounts of wine. It was a very welcome change after living for so long on short rations and it felt fantastic to be well fed. We both started to relax even though we were constantly aware of the great danger the family would be in if we were caught. The windows were shuttered and the door looked impregnable so there was no chance of anyone looking in.

The Italians heard that the 8th Army had occupied Foggia, some sixty miles to the south, and were about to push on to Termoli. While this was welcome news, they still had some way to cover before we could expect the Germans to withdraw. Peter and I discussed our plan and again decided that staying put was the best option. There were other PoWs in the village whom we would meet occasionally while taking exercise after dark and it was difficult to offer them any advice as to what to do. There were accounts of escapee PoWs being shot by the Germans and others recaptured, so the likelihood of making a successful trek south was uncertain at best. We felt that in retrospect it might have been a better option a week ago but now with so many Germans in the area it would be much more difficult to get through. I felt frustrated at our decision and envied Mac and Ricky their trek south and hoped they had managed to avoid recapture. Deep within me was a determination not to get recaptured and I suppose that strongly influenced my reluctance to attempt to trek south. It was desperately important to me to succeed and a sixty mile trek on foot over hostile territory brought too many risks of recapture while a wait of a few weeks would greatly increase the chance of success. Had I known at that time that the Gustav line was going to extend across Italy, running a few miles south of Pretoro, I would certainly have made a different decision.

Peter was also a restraining influence. He had become a very good friend and I listened to his counsel. He was very opposed to having a go and even threatened to stay in Pretoro should I decide to leave. I felt a strong obligation to get this done with him and time and again delayed decisions that in all probability should have been taken more aggressively.

Assunta Perseo was a good friend of Juliana and we were introduced to her when she visited the house. She spoke reasonable English and told us she lived with her mother and siblings in a house on the piazza opposite Gino's house. She was lively and intelligent, with an effervescent personality and great charm. She spoke of her frustration at being stuck in

Pretoro when she should have been at university in Rome and beginning her adult life away from home.

As we had to remain in our room during daylight hours the days became very long and boring. We chatted amiably and helped each other read Italian books, which in some ways was easier than trying to speak the language due to me being quite familiar with written French. Juliana produced a pack of cards, but it was different to cards found in England as it had only forty cards which meant we had to dream up new games to play. It was a pleasant diversion from tedium. I had one English book with me, *The Merchant of Venice*, and that had to sustain me throughout. I can recite the play from end to end.

The weather was changeable and noticeably cooler at night. I awoke on the morning of 12 October to torrential rain, which continued for two days and the steep streets were awash with fast running water. After a couple of days the sun returned, but the season was definitely changing. The weather would generally start fresh and sunny but by afternoon clouds would build and the crack of thunder would roll out of the mountains.

From our upstairs window we could see right up the valley, framed in the distance by the Majelletta, and while invisible to us we were told that beyond that stood Monte Focalone and the majestic Monte Acquaviva. The air was crystal clear and how tempting it was to walk out into the valley and breathe this wonderful freshness deep into our lungs. Sadly, this wasn't for us just now, although we were going to get far more than we bargained for later on.

Juliana said that in the mountains were lynx, badger and wolves. There were also wild boar, fox and hawks. She conjured images of languid summer walks through the forest with open plateaus covered in wildflowers. I was desperate to enjoy that freedom and to be able to revel in the tranquillity of walking through the forest, maybe even with the gorgeous Juliana at my side.

We would eat our breakfast and lunch in our room from a tray usually brought to us by Juliana who would stay and chat while we ate. Once dark and with the windows shuttered, we were able to join the family in their sitting room and chat in front of a log fire. We would all eat together with generous helpings of richly flavoured meats. Juliana explained that the Abruzzo region was a major producer of wine and for local people it was cheap and very good quality. The wine was dark red but without too much tannin and very drinkable. Titino was a generous host, so much so that it was rare that we didn't weave our way unsteadily up the stairs to bed. These evenings were especially soothing after the tumult of the last three years, and I began to lose focus on both the danger we were bringing to this brave family and our need to get on and escape.

Gino visited occasionally with what little news he had and spoke of life in the village. The Germans were becoming more aggressive as the 8th Army approached and there were now many more garrisoned in the lower part of the village. They were dismissive of the local people, believing the capitulation and surrender of the Italian government meant that the locals had no status at all.

He said that partisan groups were forming but felt they would be ineffective and offer little resistance. The plight of women and children was constantly on their minds and villagers were looking for ways to hide their livestock as everyone felt sure that the Germans would start stealing their food.

The Germans rarely ventured beyond the precinct of the village as the paths were steep and the area densely forested. The fascists in the village were our worst danger as they would inform the Germans where we were being hidden. Gino looked as if he would not hesitate to stand his ground and protect those he loved, but we couldn't expect him to protect us if we were discovered. In fact, we would do all we could to distance ourselves from him and the family sheltering us if there was a chance of discovery. Gino's well-worn deeply tanned face had a determined edge to it and his broad shoulders and muscular arms made him look powerful and quite dangerous. I could imagine him slipping cold steel into the heart of a German should he be forced to defend himself. I had done a bit of that when on forward patrols with the 9th Battalion in Libya. Long distance killing is one thing but the close physical presence of a man dying by your hand is an experience hard to expunge from the mind.

We were still able to get out for some air and exercise once darkness had fallen, as it was relatively safe to walk the dark streets. Even on the rare occasions we came across a German soldier, he would either ignore us or give a perfunctory wave, believing us to be villagers. While we were still in uniform the heavy winter coats lent to us hid these from German eyes. Peter's

Italian was now good enough to sound authentic and certainly adequate to bamboozle a German. We went to Gino's house on a few occasions and he introduced us to Angela Perseo, the mother of Assunta, who lived in the house opposite which had a grocery shop on its ground floor. Other than that, this life was incredibly boring for both of us and we had to work hard not to allow minor irritations to blow up into full scale arguments.

On the night of 19 October everything seemed at ease as Peter and I chatted quietly in our room before drifting off to sleep, listening to the wind outside and the occasional clatter of something dislodged by a strong gust. I was warm and comfortable having eaten another good meal, playing cards with Peter and Juliana in front of a wood fire.

At about 4am I was awoken by Juliana who, in a voice shaking with real terror, announced that the Germans were arriving in force. We had to leave immediately, otherwise if we were discovered, she and her whole family might be executed.

Carefully pulling the curtain aside in our darkened room we could just make out in the gloom that our planned escape route down a back alley behind the house was blocked by two Germans holding machine guns. There was also much commotion outside the front of the house accompanied by the deep bark of a large dog. The only other chance we had was a side window out of which we could drop about ten feet onto a roof top and then off into a side street, but Juliana told us that this was also blocked. It all seemed hopeless and Titino, Maria and Juliana looked at us with terror in their eyes.

In darkness from a window high in the house we were able to watch as a German officer started banging on the door of the house two down from where we were, and once it was ajar he flung it open and ordered his men in. About four of them entered the house with the dog straining on its leash and we were pretty certain that it was only a matter of time before they moved up the street to our house.

After several minutes, the officer reappeared and seemed to be very angry, shouting in German and eventually stomping off down the cobbled incline. The troops collected in the street then moved away and we were able to breathe again, our hearts still hammering.

We later discovered that a Fascist informer had given us away but had identified the wrong house. The family was terrified and none of us was able to sleep further that night.

Gino came by very early the next morning and told us that this informer would be found and if possible silenced. It was now too dangerous for us to remain and we had to move on immediately. We gathered our meagre belongings and said a sorrowful farewell to the brave family, hugging Maria and giving the beautiful Juliana a demure kiss on the cheek with Titino looking on with a wry smile on his face and sadness in his eyes. After this amicable sojourn it was a rude awakening being thrust back into the harshness of our situation, and maybe a good thing for it.

In the early morning light Gino took us through the back alleys to the edge of the village and we dropped onto a steep track that led down to the river about 200 feet below. He led us over the river to a rock face well screened by forest and told us that we would have to stay here during the day and he would return with food later on and take us to somewhere we could spend the night. It was a gorgeous sunny October day. The air was fresh, the water rushing past us clear and cold and the sounds of the forest echoing around us.

Having been cooped up for so long it felt tremendous to be able to walk freely and exercise legs that had become weakened from inactivity, but the recent fright made us very aware of the danger we were in and the risk we were exposing the brave Italians to. The question that we debated long and hard through the day was whether to head south or continue to wait. Again, Peter was the restraining influence, holding me back, advising caution, more and more so against my instincts.

The problem so convincingly explained by him was that the Germans had clearly established a line of defence nearby and were around in much greater numbers. Expecting to move fifty or sixty miles through occupied territory without being recaptured or killed seemed foolhardy. We agreed to stick to the plan, even with my misgivings.

Gino brought us lunch and led us downstream towards the bridge and into a peasant's house which was well screened, close to the bank. The elderly couple hastily moved us into a tiny room with bedding on the stone floor and after leaving us food and wine explained we were to remain in the room until morning. Later that evening we heard Germans looting two houses near the bridge and Gino told us the next day they had stolen jewellery. Our situation was becoming more perilous. He didn't insist that we should move on, but he clearly had misgivings about endangering another family. This didn't deter him from telling us that we were to move out of this small house and back into the village later in the day.

When the time came, we grabbed our bundles and climbed back up the track into the village and to a house owned by a chap called Armando Marcantonio, who gave us a warm friendly welcome. Armando was about my age and living on his own. The plan was to stay only one night with him and then move to Angela Perseo's house, across from Gino's own home, so he could keep an eye on things. Armando had prepared a delicious beef stew accompanied by crusty freshly baked bread, washed down with a hearty red wine. He was a bright, chatty fellow with a basic grasp of English. He spoke about his ambition to become a teacher and of his love for Pretoro, where he grew up. After a comfortable night in his small second bedroom we left early before the sun was fully up.

We made our way down the hill to the house directly opposite Gino's on the small piazza near the church. Angela Perseo, whose husband had died before the outbreak of war, had five children. She owned the local store on the ground floor of her house and needed to work very long hours to make ends meet so it must have been quite a burden feeding two extra people. The house was run by the 22-year-old Assunta whom we had already met. We were introduced to the other children, in age order, Elina, Verino, Maria and Salvatore, the youngest at 9 years. Elina was 18 and a very attractive girl, Verino 13 and Maria 11. Maria was full of excitement and energy, clearly finding adventure in the sheltering of two soldiers.

The family welcomed us with happy smiles and open arms which I felt was extraordinary given the risk they were taking. Maria and Assunta escorted us up to the top of the house where there was a pleasantly large room with two single beds and views over the valley from a small window. Our beds were comfortable, and the room felt warm so we both relaxed and chatted amicably about our recent lucky escape. While it felt wrong to put this entire family at risk, we couldn't see any other way forward other than sticking it out and remaining in the village. We felt sure the army would break through before winter set in. Assunta had explained that once into December it would snow heavily in the mountains and a deep chill would descend on the village. It was not unusual for heavy snow to fall in Pretoro and the surrounding area. Pretoro sat 2,000ft above sea level right on the edge of the Majella and winters were hard. Having absorbed this news it became clear that if the army were not able to dislodge the Germans before December not much progress was going to be made until the spring of 1944. We felt we could not stay here for another five months as it would place enormous strain on this family and local people in the village so if things got bogged down we were going to have to have a go at getting away and through the line.

Over the next few days, we were fed well and there seemed to be plenty of wine on offer at meals. Angela initially appeared to be quite a severe woman but underneath the reserved exterior she was friendly and generous. Her husband had died quite suddenly in 1934 leaving her with the five children and little money so times had been very difficult for her. We reflected on the extraordinary bravery of this woman taking in two British army officers at risk of losing her livelihood and possibly her life.

She had a general store on the ground floor accessed from the piazza with most of the produce coming from her livestock and land near the village. If not available locally she would have it brought into Pretoro from Chieti by horse and cart. It was hard subsistence living with no running water and little light, save a brief period each day when some electricity was provided. In the cellar there was an olive press and a narrow tunnel running under the road with steps leading up to a stout door opening onto it. We thought this might be a good emergency escape route, but a heavy wooden door leading to a well-screened track running down into the valley would be a better bet.

We stayed for a couple of weeks, and no doubt would have stayed much longer had our lives not been turned upside down. Life ambled on without much for us to do and boredom was our greatest challenge. Assunta was highly intelligent and bet me that she could learn English faster than I could learn Italian and I had no doubt in my mind that she would win! It had echoes of the wager made between Juliana and me a few days ago. At least this challenge kept me sane. Peter accelerated his learning with ease and they conversed together as if the language was his native one. Unhappily I made less progress.

Peter and I shared memories of our time in North Africa and the almost constant campaigning we had undertaken since arriving in late 1940. Many of my friends had been captured and some killed or wounded. The pressure on officers to conduct night-time patrols three nights out of four had been exhausting and filled with acute danger as we were expected to move into and through enemy lines to gather information. I spoke of the vicious engagements we had had against the Africa Corps and the relentless pummelling from the air and the ground. It felt good to know that Rommel had lost the battle and the Germans and Italians had been driven out of North Africa as it made the sacrifice less hard to bear. I told him about the times we had operated behind enemy lines, targeting their supply vehicles, darting in and out, using the contours of the desert to escape detection, driving at night and sometimes fighting the enemy hand to hand.

Gino told us that no-one in Pretoro knew that we were in this house and emphasised time and again that we could not show ourselves at a window or go out during the day. At night we would stretch our legs, but only after either he, Angela or Assunta had given the go-ahead. It was apparent why he was so concerned because the Germans had become more interested in the village and on occasions a couple of motorcycles with sidecars would roar up the narrow road from the church and park in the piazza, unloading their occupants to strut around the streets with that disdainful air of the ruling aggressor. He told us that they had discovered two PoWs in a house further up the hill and had cut the main supporting beams in the house making it collapse. It made me chuckle to think of the peril to the soldiers who received such an order and the risk that the house might collapse while doing the job. Less amusing was that the elderly couple who owned the house had now lost everything as a result of aiding escapees.

The Germans I was able to observe looked hardened and without compassion. I think they knew their position here was ultimately untenable given the weight of force against them and they were going to be pulverised at some point. They also knew these tough villagers hated them and they were not welcome.

When they came into the piazza we would quickly descend to the cellar via the narrow stone steps at the back of the house, knowing that one of the children would shut and lock the solid door before pulling a curtain over it. The greater danger was that should the Germans want to they could have relatively easy access to the house through the grocery store, the door of which was open all day. If they raided the house without warning, we were going to struggle to hide quickly enough.

Once the store was closed and the ground floor locked and shuttered, we felt safe and could sit with the family in the first floor sitting room. With food and wine in abundance I found myself eating and drinking far too much.

Occasionally we heard the sound of light bombing or a large explosion. Gino explained that the Germans had built a very strong defensive line about three miles south of Pretoro, cleverly using the ridges and rivers as barriers. It began to seem as if escape was just out of reach and he said that there were so many Germans in the area now it would be very difficult to get through undetected. Some escapees had tried, and their fate was uncertain, but he felt that they had probably been recaptured or shot.

On 1 November the Germans ordered the evacuation of the surrounding villages, including Rapino, a village just a few miles from Pretoro but in more gentle terrain. Many of the inhabitants came to live in Pretoro so the village population increased from 2,000 to 5,000. This placed a huge strain on resources, with food becoming scarcer. A few days later, there were many trucks on the road to Guardiagrele bringing additional Germans to the line, loaded for the return journey with villagers to ferry them north and, rumour had it, into camps.

Gino appeared to have garnered a fair amount of information from the German garrison in the village. He said that he was able to speak rudimentary German which gave him an advantage as few, if any, villagers spoke German, and this meant he was useful to them. He was told that it was General Kesselring who commanded the German forces extending across Italy in a line from about fifty miles north of Naples to the mouth of the Sango River in the east. There were three or four divisions in place this side of the Apennines and their job was to prevent the Allied army from breaking through and sweeping west from the Adriatic coast, thus encircling German troops defending the line north of Naples. He wasn't certain of the troops in this theatre of war but had heard that a 'General Heirdrich' commanded this eastern sector and he had a Panzer division at his disposal. Gino felt that the terrain with its rivers, gorges and mountains presented a considerable challenge to the Allies as the corridor running between the mountains and the coast was narrow.

He predicted that the Germans would eventually use Pretoro more fully as it commanded excellent views over the valleys lying to the south and to the east as far as the sea.

That night we heard the sound of heavy guns thundering for several hours to the south-east of Pretoro and later learnt that it was the British attacking Vasto, about thirty miles away. Tantalizingly close now but so far away with 80,000 German troops between us and the Allies.

In the house, little Maria had a beautiful voice and the sound of her singing would bring a freshness to our dull lives. One song in particular struck a chord with me and that was *Il Vento* which had been adapted to become the song of the resistance in Italy. Its words captured the spirit of the Italian partisans' fight against the fascists, a song of strength of heart and harsh revenge. It was a song little Maria and her family could sing with pride for they were the glorious heart of Italy and its people.

A few days later the sight of Allied planes flying low over the village gave us renewed hope. German vehicles were bunched below us on the bridge and beyond and the British aircraft caused massive panic. It was great to see Hans and Fritz scattering in terror, even though the planes didn't press an attack, probably for fear of collateral damage. However, the amount of activity going on and the proximity of our forces heralded a fundamental change to our cosy lives.

That afternoon two motorcycles with sidecars and a staff car drove into the piazza. From our small top floor window we could see a pompous looking kraut emerge, with polished jackboots and a stick to slap his thigh with. The soldiers in the motorcycles spread out with guns at the ready and the whole thing looked very menacing.

The officer banged on the door demanding immediate entrance and Peter and I hastily gathered our few belongings. Assunta had just come in to take our lunch tray downstairs and went quickly out hoping to reach the kitchen before the door was opened but Elina was already there, and the officer marched in barking incomprehensible instructions.

He didn't react in any way to Assunta appearing on the stairs with the tray, so she was able to move quickly to the kitchen. The situation was dire as he spoke some Italian and said he wanted to look at the house with a view to billeting a couple of officers and proceeded to march up the stairs to the first floor. Luckily that was as far as he went. He appeared to have made a decision that he was going to use the house and left to get his officers.

Peter and I went down the stairs into the cellar as there was no chance of making a break for it while the soldiers were still so close. The Germans returned and went to the top of the house and into the room we had vacated a few minutes before. We were stuck in the cellar all that afternoon and into the night and for a time had to listen to the Germans singing a song: 'England, England, you are bound to lose the war'. Ha, I thought, you will all be singing a lament soon enough. Possibly rather foolishly we decided we would sing as well.

We were desperate to get out, but the risk to the family was far too great if we were discovered. Things quietened down at about 11pm and Assunta came into the cellar with Armando to say that she felt it was now safe enough for us to leave the house and go down the steep steps behind Gino's house which would bring us to the edge of the village. She felt it wasn't safe to use the door to the valley side of the house as Germans had been seen patrolling this area at night, and the two officers were now sleeping in our room with its window looking out over the valley.

She then pulled aside the curtain and opened the low door through which we crept into a tunnel carved out of rock and that brought us to the other side of the narrow road running from the church to the piazza. We crept silently up the steps and opened a stout wooden door to the road just twenty or so yards from the piazza, where we noticed several German vehicles parked in the small square. We peered into the darkness of the unlit street and it appeared there were no guards on duty. We moved silently around to the side of Gino's house and down precipitous steps leading to a narrow alleyway that sloped gently down to the edge of the village. Here we waited anxiously in the shadows to make sure there were no Germans guarding this entrance to the village. Armando signalled us to follow and led us down a steep, rutted track into the woods until we came to a small cave well screened by trees. He had put blankets in the cave and said that Gino would come by early in the morning to move us as this cave was not going to be adequate to shield us from prying eyes and the weather. We bedded down, comfortable enough on a deep mattress of leaves, and warmed by our blankets soon slept.

Chapter 11

Cave life

At first light the next morning Gino appeared with food and said that he would arrange for couriers to bring us food each day. He beckoned us to follow him, so we gathered our blankets and spare clothes and moved to the other side of the track, climbing slightly back towards the village. He led us to an excellent cave, tucked deep into the steep hillside with tangled vegetation hanging down from the ledge above and enough trees and plants to conceal the narrow path to it.

The cave was in two parts, one quite spacious area and the other a small ante-room accessed through an arch. It looked as though it had been worked on in the past as it was a perfect hiding place. The only problem was a lack of height which meant that neither of us was able to stand upright. It would be possible to light a small fire each evening without concern about discovery and this was a blessing now that the evenings were getting cold.

Gino left us saying he would return with extra blankets, and some buckets so we could drop into the valley to fetch water from the river. When he returned, he also brought matches, kindling wood and food for the evening. He encouraged us to forage for berries and mushrooms in the valley. I asked about the Germans coming into the valley to search for escapees and he replied that as yet they had shown no interest in doing so, but added that this would not necessarily remain the case. The path up to the village was well concealed and after a steep climb it brought one to a back alley from which there were various routes in. While we very rarely ventured back into the village, it was the route taken by the couriers to bring food.

We settled into our new home as it was clear that we would be here for a while. Returning to the village was going to be very risky now that the Germans had taken up residence. Later in the day the sun fell behind Monte d'Ugni and as soon as it had disappeared it became cold, making me realise that it was going to get quite harsh as winter progressed. Peter went out and collected fallen wood. There was plenty, and we lit a small fire in the mouth of the smaller cave which kept us surprisingly warm and created a ghostly atmosphere with the flames flickering off the limestone walls, casting deep shadows into the interior. Gino had brought a small supply of candles but suggested using these very sparingly so most of the time we sat huddled around the fire, talking in hushed tones.

Our first courier arrived the next morning. A smiling Maria carried a basket draped with a cloth under which there was dried meat, some cheese and cooked pasta. There was also a loaf of freshly baked bread which smelt amazing, a couple of apples and a generous flagon of red wine. She had also brought plates and cutlery which we were to keep. She stayed with us for an hour or so, chatting nineteen to the dozen in Italian so I could only nod and look as if I understood every word.

It was safe enough for us to wander up the valley as superficially there was little to distinguish us from the Italians living in the village and the Germans rarely ventured here. The exercise was welcome, and we met a number of other PoWs, all living in caves and numbering about fifteen. At a guess I would think most of these got recaptured. I told Peter that it was now we should make our escape. We were fit and healthy having been fed well over the preceding month and more importantly were becoming an unacceptable burden on our Italian hosts. Food was becoming more and more scarce, given the number of mouths to feed in the village. Peter again vociferously argued that we should not risk all we had achieved this close to making a success of it. He felt that the 8th Army would force a breach in the German defensive line before Christmas and was adamant that he would not join me should I decide to go. My loyalty to him overcame my desire to get on with it. I knew I had more determination than him and felt protective of him, almost as if he was under my command and I needed to make sure he got out.

On one of Maria's visits she said Assunta would not be able to come to the cave as there was too much risk of her being detected whereas an 11-year-old child generated little interest. Verino would share the courier work and we should expect them once each day. Peter seemed very disappointed that he was not going to see Assunta, making me realise that they had formed quite an attachment. He was liable to be rather reckless and I worried that he might try to get back into the village to see her without consideration for their safety.

A couple of evenings later my fears were realised. He drank too much wine and, filled with bravado, decided to go into the village. This was a crazy risk to take as there were many more Germans in the town than a few days earlier. He shrugged off my plea for caution and disappeared into the night. It wasn't long before he returned saying that he did get to the track running close to the Perseo house and almost ran straight into two Germans on sentry duty. Luckily they were smoking and the faint breeze had brought the smell to him in time for him to stop and quietly retrace his steps.

After being cooped up for so long, grumpy about our itinerant life and generally fed up with the whole thing I lost my temper with him and we spent the next day or so in sullen resentment, hardly talking and both acting like children. Later the following evening we settled our pointless squabble, and over a cup or two of the local wine we reflected on how well we had got on during past months with very few fall-outs.

Peter was always the cheerleader and had an agreeably optimistic approach to our life in the village and hills. Through all of this though, I wasn't certain that, come the day of reckoning when we would have to make our final bid for freedom, he would have it in him to get through. His bonhomie and carefree attitude hid a lack of real determination; real grit when the chips were down.

The children came to the cave each day, which eased the terrible boredom we felt. We had to be extremely careful as the Germans had now begun to send men into the valley, probably on reconnaissance missions. Gino told us that a number of PoWs had been caught and that a couple of villagers had been arrested and taken away for sheltering escapees. Our hiding in the cave meant that it would be unlikely any family could be accused of aiding us.

The weather took a severe turn for the worse, with heavy rain and intermittent sleet. This area of Italy has more than its fair share of snow and we could see snow settling higher up the valley. The temperature had dropped into the thirties and a bitter wind whistled down the valley.

The river swelled as waters cascaded off the high peaks and our cave was filled with its noise. The problem with outdoor living was that, once cold, it was almost impossible to get warm again. Getting wet was something we tried to avoid at all costs as our clothes would remain damp for many days.

As we moved deeper into November, the days shrunk in length and the gloom pervaded our hovel. The trees had lost their leaves and the cover protecting our cave became wispy and fragile. Gino brought more warm clothes and we kept the fire alight all day and well into the evening. We had built a rock wall on the open side of the cave in front of the fire to prevent it being seen by anyone in the valley. It meant more smoke blew into the cave and made life even more uncomfortable. We would also heat rocks in the fire and use these for warmth when settling down for the night.

The children stopped acting as couriers and were replaced by two swarthy Italians called Rocka and Enio, and Gino brought what news he had of the war. The Allies were now very close, having a defensive line half a mile further south than the German line. He said that a Canadian division was in our section as well as some British paratroopers supplemented by a brigade of New Zealanders.

We also heard that the Germans had a Polish regiment which had been pressed into service on the line. The British also had a Polish Regiment made up of those who had managed to escape Poland. The Poles were reluctant to fire on each other and many of them had deserted the German line and gone across to the British. So many in fact that the Polish regiment had been withdrawn from the line.

As time went on, less and less food was brought to us and Gino told us that the Germans were looting livestock and raiding supplies hidden in houses. This was tightening the noose of despair within the village and life had become very hard. While the villagers were clever at finding places to hide their cattle, turncoat informers, usually fascist sympathisers, would direct the Germans with the expectation that they would be well fed for doing so. Gino's eyes became deadly dark when speaking of this and I guessed these informants would suffer a well-deserved fate one dark night. There were plenty of places to hide a body in the hills with no chance of discovery.

Our day was occasionally interrupted by artillery shells landing a few hundred yards away. We assumed that the bridge was a practice target and the deep crump of an explosion fizzed up what would normally be a day of intense boredom. Each and every day I felt the urge to have a go at moving on and letting fate decide our lives, but Peter held me back saying that we had come so far why risk it all on the home stretch. However, what I did begin to do was walk out into the valley at first light and climb the steep tracks as high as time would allow before the risk of discovery was too great. I knew that sooner or later we were going to have to have a go at getting through and the terrain here was going to make that very arduous indeed. After a couple of weeks Gino cautioned me and said that with the number of Germans now in the area I should take great care, so we were confined to our cave for much of the time.

Most days our food was bread, dried fruits, cheese, milk, figs, nuts and an occasional apple. We were given small lumps of bad meat on two days only for the month between mid-November and December. Peter became very ill with an acute bout of dysentery lasting several days which weakened him badly. I suffered too but managed to throw it off after a couple of days, although it had a habit of returning and I wasn't able to shake it off for many months. Our clothes were now infested with fleas as was the straw and leaves we slept on and there was nothing we could do about it.

As we were largely confined to the cave during the day, our brief forays into the valley were to collect water, and there was never enough to wash with, so we began to smell of the earth. Early on I had occasionally gone down to the river when it was very dark and try to wash but it was almost not worth the bother as the slope down was very steep and it was too easy to trip and fall. I dreamt about hot coffee. My physical condition began to deteriorate and I noticed the effort of carrying water from the river to the cave was leaving me short of breath.

Chapter 12

The villagers leave their village

Enio had told us that the Germans were coming into the village in greater numbers and that there was talk that at some point soon all the villagers would be rounded up and sent away to camps allowing the Germans to have absolute control of the village. Already the villagers who had come to Pretoro from Rapino had been shepherded into trucks and driven away. Gino confirmed this and told us that a number of the villagers would prefer to leave the village on their own terms and risk all by living in the mountains, even in the midst of winter, rather than submit to captivity. To this end preparations were already in train to move livestock and fodder into caves high in the Majella and store what surplus food they had. From early December onwards there had been a quiet exit from the village as these people gradually moved out of their homes carrying with them blankets and warm clothing.

On 10 December Gino came into the cave and said that the Germans were arriving in force. He said that they had made Pretoro their headquarters and were putting into effect plans to evacuate all villagers into camps near Chieti, and those villagers who had not left were being rounded up. He estimated that of the 2,000 living in Pretoro, about 400 had taken the decision to escape into the mountains. He said that his compatriots had identified caves suitable to house groups of families, of which there are many in the hills, had stored supplies and moved cattle into well concealed caves with enough fodder to keep them alive for several weeks. There was plenty of water cascading off the hills that was easy to collect. He said the Germans were coming into the valley trying to find cattle, so it was going to be a battle to protect them from looting.

Food would be even more limited, and Gino advised that it would be safer for us to move deeper into the hills as it was no longer possible for Enio and Rocka to come this close to the village. If we went further away from the village, we would have more freedom to move around and forage for fungi and berries. It was clear from the way he spoke that we would have to make a decision quite soon and he could only support us for a short while longer. He also talked of where we might make our bid for freedom, talking of the defensive line running from Ortona in the north to Pennapiedimonte in the southwest and beyond. The closest point to allied forces would be from Pennapiedimonte but the journey to get there over the mountains was rugged and quite dangerous in places, with deep impenetrable gorges. An easier route would be to the north of Pennapiedimonte but difficult to avoid capture as it was a strong defensive position for the Germans, with no risk to them from a flanking attack due to the terrain. The safer route was to the south but the journey to get there was much more challenging as it would mean finding our way up and down very steep slopes, and the going was very tough, with three ridge climbs of 2,500 feet each. The snow was now well established high in the mountains and fell frequently a couple of thousand feet below the high ridges lying at about 6,000ft.

Peter and I gathered our things and tied them into bundles, and in the afternoon, with a few hours to go before darkness set in, we moved away from our home for the past month or so, descended the steep path leading down to the river and followed its course upstream to where we were to meet Gino. After half an hour or so we arrived at a ford and he greeted us with a couple of swarthy Italians who grunted a welcome before turning towards the hills and our journey to the Col D'Angelo which was a climb of about 1000ft though densely wooden terrain. After an hour and a half of straining our unfit limbs up zig-zag tracks we came to a deep low cave under a sheer rockface which was to be our home for the next week. We would have plenty of warning if Germans were to come this far into the hills and good places close by to hide. We were able to light a fire and sat huddled around it eating a few slices of bread and some dried figs. Hunger was a constant companion now and probably our greatest enemy.

One bright light in this very dark tunnel was that with our newly found freedom we could again make contact with the Perseo family, who were living in a large cave nearby shared with about fifty villagers. Assunta was in surprisingly good form given how bitterly cold and wet it was. Angela looked daunted by the task ahead of her which had been hard enough in the village. She spoke of her concern for the health of her children and what she was expected to do if one of them became very ill. Food was adequate for the moment but with an exasperated shrug and a waving of arms she surmised that this could go on for many months and the privations they would suffer could make life intolerable. She swore furiously at the Germans and their awful arrogance. She cursed them for bringing such grief and toil to the village and more generally to Italy and the world. She had been a young woman during the First World War when Italy had fought alongside the Allies against Germany and Austria. She remembered the awful toll exacted on the Italians just a short breath of time ago and couldn't believe this conflict hadn't sated the lust for dominance so apparent in German nature. After a moment of silence, she collected herself and stood up from the boulder she had been sitting on and with a wan smile walked away with drooping shoulders. I didn't see her again, this wonderful strong woman of the Majella who was as brave as a lion and as enduring as an Arctic Tern.

Elina came to visit us a few times as did the excitable and energetic Maria, who found it to be a great adventure. We would sit outside the cave safe from view from below due to the density of the forest and the very steep slope. A cliff rose some fifty feet behind us on top of which was dense undergrowth affording good protection from someone viewing from above. The precocious Salvatore was an infrequent visitor but when he came he took great delight attempting to speak English. Even at such a young age he spoke of wishing to become a teacher when he grew up. He had an inquisitive mind and was keen to learn about our lives in England and how they compared with his in Italy. I told him I had previously left my home address with Assunta with an open invitation for any member of the family to stay, hoping I might be there to greet them.

We met many of the other villagers dotted around the mountain living in caves, looking forlorn and desperate in the cold. Without anything else to do for most of the time we sat huddled in our cave, shivering under a blanket, watching the rain and sleet lash down into the forest.

Food was now very scarce as the villagers could no longer afford to share much of what they had. I felt we had become an irritating encumbrance and they wished we would go. In the last week we had chiefly eaten bread, cheese and milk. Otherwise our diet was supplemented by small amounts of pasta, dried figs, nuts and an occasional apple. I was constantly hungry, cold and depressed. Peter was suffering again with bad dysentery and my attack kept on returning which made us both weaker.

On 22 December I had a reckoning with Peter. Our health was deteriorating, we were a burden on the Italians and before long we were going to get recaptured. We had to throw the dice now and make a break for it. Peter again argued strongly against moving across the mountains in mid-winter but I was having none of it. After a heated exchange it was with some reluctance he agreed I was right and we had to give it a go.

Gino came to the cave and after hearing of our decision said that Ezio would come to the cave at dawn the next morning, after going high into the mountains to find a suitable cave for us to use. It was too risky for us to wander around trying to find a cave as there were Italian spies about who would give us away. He had drawn a rough map of our route which had us moving west, climbing firstly the ridge above us.

We hoped that we would be able to see the British line from a high ridge and plan how we might cross. I felt excited that we were now going to have a go come what may but sensed that Peter harboured a deep reluctance. He seemed to have lost his enthusiasm and no matter what I said to him he wasn't able to jolt himself out of his melancholy. The five weeks of cave dwelling had taken its toll on him to such an extent that I again felt that when the time came he wouldn't make it.

We were ready to go at dawn but there was no Ezio. At about 9am, Peter said he was going to head off to try and find Gino and get the latest information as we had heard much shouting echoing up the valley. We couldn't see anything because there was a dense mist hanging in the trees. It was encouraging that Peter took this initiative and he seemed happier now we were definitely going to move on.

Half an hour later I heard many German voices very close by but still was unable to see anything because of the mist. I swept leaves over our clothes and blankets in case they came to the cave and prepared to hide at the back of the cave in a shallow recess should the voices come any closer. I was nervous and twitchy, wondering whether after all this time I would allow myself to be recaptured or make a run for it. Running for it in this terrain was not easy as off the tracks the slopes were far too steep and on the track too good a target.

The sound of machine gun fire and rifle shots echoed around the valley and I could hear screams from further down the hill. Worryingly there was no sign of Peter.

A couple of hours later, I spotted two German helmets below me and scurried to the deep, dark recess in the cave and lay down on the ledge with my face turned to the wall. The soldiers came into the cave but failed to notice me lying there with my heart hammering expecting at any moment to be challenged. It was an extraordinary moment. The Germans were only ten yards from me but they didn't see me, that is how close I came to being recaptured. They talked together for a short while before leaving the cave and moving away.

A little later Gino appeared from the mist which was still shrouding the trees. He was a powerful man but moved like a cat and seemed to be able to materialise without warning. I told him about my near capture experience, and he confirmed there appeared to be a major German push to round people up. He said that they were shepherding the Italian men they found in caves and moving them to the river close to Pretoro. Their intent was unknown but some trying to flee had been brutally rounded up. He had not seen Peter and was annoyed that he had gone into the valley. He had brought a generous portion of meat, some bread and a lump of cheese to aid our escape and I knew this to be quite a sacrifice, given the difficulty the villagers were facing. I thanked him for this and for all he had done for us. He looked at me with sadness in his eyes and wished me success in our venture. He knew I would not be returning. What a remarkable man he was.

Not long after Gino left, Peter crawled back into the cave with a wide grin on his face. He had been captured but not recognised as an Englishman and, by offering to help some Italians escape, had managed to slip away. His adventure had done him the world of good and he was gung-ho about getting away.

The rest of the day was spent quietly in the cave listening to the depressing noise of wailing women and children. The Germans had taken the Italian men they had found away to an unknown fate, looted all the cattle they could find and torched two of the larger caves and we listened to the crackle of the fires. My loathing of them increased. It was as if these poor Italians no longer had any identity.

The family home Folyats, Fyfield, Essex in 1938.

Tony Hough, Zermatt in 1938, checking out the brandy supplies.

Above left: Tony Hough, Zermatt 1938.

Above right: David Stirling waiting to embark on a ship to France with 5th Battalion Scots Guards on their way to Chamonix.

5th Battalion Scots Guards, Chamonix, February 1940. Oswald (Mickey) Rooney (front, right) became a great post-war friend.

5th Battalion, Chamonix, February 1940.

Time for a fag and cuppa. B Company 9th Battalion in Libya, 1941.

Time for members of the platoon to rest. Tony Hough is seated in shadow, back right.

Messy business maintaining the carriers. Tony Hough's platoon, B Company 9th Battalion, Libya, 1941.

Playtime in the desert. B Company 9th Battalion.

9th Battalion manoeuvring in the desert battle of November 1942.

Right: Gerald Hough at the water tower in which Tony Hough hid for three days. Chieti camp, 2017.

Below: Chieti camp in 2017. Now home to the Italian Military Police.

Above: Pretoro, seemingly glued to the hillside.

Left: Gino Francioni's house as it was before renovation.

Angela Perseo, a most determined woman who intimidated the most resolute of Germans.

Looking up to Perseo house, top right.

The Perseo house on the piazza, Pretoro. Hough sheltered in top floor.

Looking east towards the sea from the piazza Pretoro.

The cave lying twenty metres below the village where Hough and Gunn hid for a month.

The cave was well screened by vegetation. The wall to hide the fire is still in place.

Above left: The endless maze of narrow streets in Pretoro.

Above right: Well concealed steps leading up towards the church and piazza, Pretoro.

Above left: Narrow alley and house in Pretoro looking towards the valley.

Above right: View down the gorge towards Pennapiedimonte. It has to be crossed at the upper end as lower down is impassable.

Left: View up the gorge from nearby Pennapiedimonte.

Above left: Major Anthony Hough, 1946.

Above right: Major Anthony Hough in a 'devil may care' pose, 1946.

Below left: Germany, 1946.

Below right: Germany, 1946.

Above: A happy day, July 1946. They say a wet wedding is an enduring one, and this time it was right.

Left: Peter Gunn, 1952, on route to the south of France with Tony.

Casa Mila today. Previously the home of Gino Francioni.

The Perseo house in the foreground and Casa Mila in the background.

Verino (88) and Maria (86) Perseo, siblings in 2017. Still energetic and agile.

Verino Perseo, now 88 years old.

Right: Maria Perseo, a youthful 86 years old.

Below: View up the valley from Casa Mila, Pretoro. This is the valley many of the villagers escaped to in December 1943.

Above: One of the caves in the Majella Mountains used by the villagers in December 1943.

Left: Hidy hole in a cave, used to protect supplies from German eyes.

Author, Gerald Hough.

Chapter 13

Time to go

On Christmas Eve we set off from our cave an hour before dawn. The going was difficult in the dark, but we needed to be clear of the cave dwellings and prying eyes before light. It was raining hard making the ground greasy, so great care had to be taken to avoid straining an ankle. The track was frequently blocked by fallen beech trees and the route around quite hazardous, with sheer drops onto jagged rocks. A broken leg now would destroy all hopes of escape, even if one were to survive the fall.

As it began to get light, we found many Apennine salamanders on the path with their distinctive bright orange spots and flat heads. My legs felt tired almost from the outset and I knew it was my mental strength that was going to get me there rather than physical. I was wet and cold, even with the hard slog up the mountain. I had hoped we would meet some partisans on the mountain who would help direct us, but none appeared. However, when we reached a ridge above the Camino valley, we met two Italian men who were trying to avoid the Germans below us. The Germans were still hunting for Italians and continuing their looting.

We climbed high into the mountain and the sound of shouts of despair and hard German commands faded behind us. It was a gloomy December day with mist shrouding the trees and bitterly cold. We climbed to about 5,000ft with the rain turning to snow and ice, making the going quite treacherous. After a while we came across a group of Rapino people living in a large cave where they had a welcoming fire to warm ourselves by. They told us that they had been living here since Rapino was evacuated a month or so before and they looked pretty desperate with little food and a mule foraging for what it could find on the broken, snow covered ground outside the cave.

Their generosity was extraordinary, and they gave us a little to eat and a bowl of a broth made from fungi. I sat with the hot bowl warming my hands sipping this unfathomable brew hoping it wouldn't result in terrible stomach cramps. I took off my wet outer clothes and hung them to dry close to the fire with a dry blanket given to me to ward off the chill. I don't know how we would have fared without meeting these kind and generous people.

They told us that four British officers and an Italian girl had stayed in a branch and leaf shelter tucked into a cranny just outside the cave and they had left a couple of days before to try and cross the line. They suggested the best way for us to cross was north of Pennapiedimonte but warned us that it was very difficult to get across and many trying had not made it. Now dryer and warmed by the fire, Peter and I moved out of the cave into the small shelter used by the others and lit a fire around which we curled for warmth and tried, without much success, to sleep. The snow had stopped falling and the skies had cleared leaving us with the brilliance of a night sky filled to the brim with stars. The temperature had dropped another few degrees, and the cold invaded every part of my malnourished body.

Peter's normally cheery demeanour was missing, and he had become sullen and uncommunicative which I put down to the constant cold and gnawing hunger. I tried hard to encourage him out if it, talking of our imminent escape from the clutch of the Germans and return to England, but something was missing. I thought that the risk we might not manage to stay alive for much longer had got to him. He had become overly reflective and possibly lost his focus. He was a brave and resourceful man who had been a great friend over the last months and I wanted to finish this with him. After a long while I fell into a fitful sleep, the icy clutch of the night embracing me ever more firmly.

My eyes flickered open as light slowly brought Christmas Day 1943 into our rough shelter. The fire had died during the night and there wasn't a part of me that wasn't frozen. At a guess I would estimate the temperature to have been 5 degrees below zero and here we were with little food and poorly clothed. It was tempting to throw the cards in and go back down into the valley and let the Germans take us. I was able to push these thoughts aside and didn't mention my doubts to Peter, who was shivering uncontrollably while trying to relight the fire.

As the fire crackled and spat to life Peter seemed to pick himself up and became more cheerful, talking animatedly about heading across the mountains and skirting the main concentration of Germans near Pennapiedimonte and Rapino. Their line was apparently thinner to the south-west of Pennapiedimonte as the terrain was much more challenging and steep mountain slopes rising to Monte d'Ugni made it nigh on impossible for the Allies to flank attack the German positions.

He then told me he had decided to go back into the valley to get food and information, which made me wonder whether this had enervated him. I didn't agree, and we argued for a while as I couldn't see the point of it. In my view, we had to make a break for it before we became too weak, and we had all the information we were likely to get. Even though I had felt a similar temptation I firmly believed that returning to the valley would put him at risk of capture and possibly worse. At least from our base we were positioned for our escape. We argued heatedly and he became quite agitated, adamant that he would descend into the valley and return later that day. He left his blanket with me before shaking my hand and saying that he would see me back here before sundown.

As his shape disappeared into the light cloud hanging over the valley, I felt a sense of doom and somehow knew I would not see him again. Left on my own, cold and hungry, I began to think that maybe he was right, and the easier path was to delay. But to join him would have meant risking recapture and losing the chance to determine our own fate. To let it go after all we had been through seemed nonsense, especially because of the brave families and in particular Gino's efforts to keep us out of German hands.

I couldn't stop shivering in the intense cold. I managed to dry my clothes over the fire and waited in vain for Peter to return. As the early fall of darkness approached there was no welcoming sign of my great friend with his infectious good spirit appearing over the ridge and I knew he wouldn't return that night. I had spent last Christmas in the cramped confines of a hot, smelly Italian submarine and this one was even worse, freezing on the side of a mountain slowly starving to death. At least in the submarine it had been warm.

Christmas was 'celebrated' eating three slices of bread and drinking a cup of water warmed by the fire.

My sleep was again fitful that night, plagued by nightmares of action in Libya and the gruesome deaths of soldiers both English and Italian. The wind had picked up through the night and I felt snowflakes landing gently on my cheek, blown through the thin canopy of leaves. I awoke to find there was twelve inches of snow on the ground and it was still snowing heavily, so most depressingly there seemed little chance that Peter would make it back unless it stopped. I built up the fire and huddled against it for warmth without much to do other than wait.

There was a commotion in the cave next to my meagre shelter and I looked out to see the Rapino people load up their mule with their scanty possessions. They told me they were going to descend into the valley as it was too cold and miserable to remain this high. With great generosity they gave me bread and a slice of cheese which went some way to alleviate my hunger.

I moved our bundles into the cave they had vacated and stoked up the fire they had left in its small rock circle, but it was still impossible to get warm. The snowstorm cleared and a watery sun appeared briefly, reflecting off the cloud lying lower in the valley. The peaks came into view, brilliant in their snow-clad splendour and for a time I sat and reflected on my skiing trips before the war, my joining the Tower Hamlets Rifles, the journey to Switzerland and climbing Monte Rosa with the exhilarating ski down through deep virgin snow, and then the extraordinary trip out to Chamonix with the Snowballers in February 1940. It all seemed a lifetime ago, and in a world where I was much more carefree. What a journey it had been, and here I am sitting in a cave 6,000 feet up a mountain in late December 1943 freezing my bollocks off and acutely hungry. I imagined myself successfully passing through the Allied line and tucking into an enormous plate of fried food with two fingers raised towards Germany and the bastards who had put me through all this.

The cloud thickened before long and gloom descended once again, bringing me back to the present. Still no sign of Peter and I began to think that he had decided to remain in the valley or had been recaptured. I doubted he would just stay there without coming to tell me but felt he may have decided that the heavy snow made the climb back up too difficult.

I slept the night in the cave, sheltered from the wind but still very cold, even when wrapped in both mine and Peter's blankets. As dawn came, I decided I had to go as I could not survive another night without food high in the mountains. I resolved to try to get across south of Pennapiedimonte as the ridges were too high to its north and with the snow it would be too treacherous and cold. This meant I had to cross over two ridges, Lago dell'Orso and Campanaro. Walking in the snow was going to be very challenging. The terrain was also acutely dangerous. There were narrow indistinct tracks leading down very steep slopes and any unplanned detour might bring one to the edge of a precipice with a drop of several hundred feet. Given the ice and snow it would be all too easy to slip and that would be it. Even the beech-clad slopes were so steep that a fall could be lethal. The other problem was being able to find my way. At least once I got to the gorge, I would know that I should follow it downstream to the south of Pennapiedimonte.

Once the decision to go had been made I felt a strong sense of exhilaration which gave me a surge of strength in my legs. I climbed to the top of the ridge about two hundred feet above me with my feet and shins sinking into the soft snow with every step making it difficult and tiring. It felt as if my body had long since decided it didn't have the fuel to continue and it was only my determination to keep going that made me lift one foot after the other to propel myself forward. Having crested the ridge on this gloomy morning, with cloud obscuring the tree filled slope below, I dropped into the first valley, and after about five hundred feet the snow thinned out and I was able to follow a narrow track through the trees into the valley floor. I then began the climb up towards Campanaro, still amongst close growing beech and fir, with plenty of fern on the ground. The cloud descended into the valley and wrapped its cold embrace around my shoulders, obscuring much and helping me a little.

As I climbed, I heard voices and crouched behind a large rockfall. Two German troopers and an Italian walked by within yards of where I crouched without noticing me and were rapidly lost to sight in the dense forest clinging to these very steep slopes. My heart pounded as I reminded myself that I was not alone on these mountains and I had to remain alert at all times. When working hard to climb it was all too easy to focus entirely on the effort and lose awareness of what was going on around. At least the Germans travelled in pairs or more and made quite a noise.

On approaching the top of Campanaro I came across a cave inhabited by some people from Pennapiedimonte who had a good fire going and a cabbage broth on the boil. We sat together, and I was able to understand enough to learn that crossing the line was very difficult and many trying had been unsuccessful. They generously gave me some of the warming broth to drink and a few slices of surprisingly fresh bread and this was enough to bolster my flagging spirit.

Having rested here for an hour or so I left feeling cheerful and determined. I dropped into the second valley and started the climb to reach the top of La Rapina which was a good slog up a steep slope of about two thousand feet, which I found very tiring. For the last 500 feet or so I was again walking on ice and snow making the way treacherous in places. As I walked the mist lifted and a weak December sun filtered through the trees creating pretty contrasts of light and dark. I made it in about two hours and, from an excellent vantage point high on the ridge, was able to see Guardiagrele and the British Line. What joy I felt at seeing the line at last and knowing that I was within a few miles of making a successful escape. My determination to get through grew. To get caught now would be unbearable. With great care I dropped into the valley running to the south-west of Pennapiedimonte following the route that Gino had mapped out. The gorge running down to Pennapiedimonte was impassable as too steep, so I had to cross the narrow valley higher up, climb again several hundred feet, still heading west, before turning south and dropping steeply. It was easy to lose the narrow tracks down as one rock looks pretty much like another and I frequently had to climb back to find the route. After an hour or so I met two Italians who proved to be friendly and with their basic English and my basic Italian we managed to communicate well enough for them to tell me that they were going to try and make a break across the line that night and they pointed out a route for me to follow saying it seemed to be the best way through.

The wind had increased and the temperature had fallen several degrees so again I started to shiver in the biting cold even with my hard walking. There was no going back as I had neither the energy nor means of getting across the high ridges. That was no longer an option.

I tried to watch the wind direction to give me a bearing, but the clouds seemed to be blowing in a different direction to the wind on the ground, so I supposed that it was swirling against the slopes of the valley and the clouds were a better indicator. I rested a while and set off at dusk for the final effort to get across the line. I was fearful about having got this far only to fall at the last fence.

Chapter 14

Across the line

I pushed on down the valley skirting Pennapiedimonte rising steeply about half a mile away up the hillside on my left, and then tracked swiftly along quite easy ground close by the Avello river. I came to a narrow dirt road running down the valley with open terrain on both sides making finding cover difficult. The skies had cleared and a weak moon cast light on the valley. To my left I spotted Germans about a hundred yards away, but it was too far to make anything out clearly. The excitement of the moment increased in me making me feel happier than at any time over the last year.

Moving cautiously down the road I was brought to a sudden stop when two Germans came out of the brush to my left and walked ahead of me down the valley. After a brief moment to recover from the shock, I thought the best thing to do was to follow them and hope they didn't turn around. After about two hundred yards I veered right off the track at the place I had viewed from higher up and climbed a steep bank to bring me alongside the German line.

My position was very dangerous at this point because, if spotted, I would most certainly be shot as it was unlikely I would successfully respond to a challenge. There was a group of German soldiers behind me in a small house talking and I could smell their cigarette smoke. I went on, crossing over a field communications wire and came to another dirt road. On my left, just twenty-five yards away, there were more Germans, but to my right it seemed to be clear. I crawled across the dirt track and then walked in a crouch with no obstacles to hinder my progress and no sign of any Germans, but I knew they had to be close.

The terrain became very difficult and going forward was a real struggle. There were steep muddy banks all around me and the slippery clay made moving across them very near impossible. I slipped and rolled in the mud trying desperately to make progress, but the effort sapped my energy.

It was thirsty work and I had to resort to drinking muddy water to keep myself going. After three hours of this I came to an exhausted halt, unable to go any further. But the moment I stopped the ferocious cold gripped me again and I knew that if I curled into a ball to sleep I might never awaken. I had to keep moving, so every ten minutes I would get up and do a half-minute of exercise to try and generate warmth. Eventually overtaken by exhaustion, I slumped into a hollow and slept for an hour, with the mud coating me probably keeping me alive. Heavy guns had been firing but then fell silent.

On 28 December the sky brightened in the east just about where I had wanted it to be, so I knew roughly the direction I should take. I found myself close to the river and had no option other than to slip quietly into the icy water and wade downstream. The pre-dawn gloom gave me cover, otherwise I would have been easy to spot. After about ten minutes I heard German voices on the bank above me and realised that I was perilously close to their line. I gasped as I crouched closer to the water and the ice cold of it sucked the remaining heat from me and my body began to shudder at the shock of it. I moved as quietly as I could under their position, made more difficult by my sinking knee-deep into gluey mud. To make progress I had to flatten my body onto the water which soaked me and brought more bouts of shivering. I could see the long barrel of a field gun sticking over the bank of the river and I passed quietly under it, again smelling cigarette smoke and hearing the occasional clink of metal against metal.

After moving about a quarter mile downstream, now shivering uncontrollably, I saw a small decrepit house near to the bank and I clawed my way out, approaching it cautiously, seeing smoke coming from the chimney. Inside were an Italian couple who refused my request for food and warned me that the Germans were very close and I should continue down the river. I found it odd that this couple were living bang next door to the line and in danger of being taken out by artillery fire at any moment. They were keen for me to leave immediately but thankfully didn't raise an alarm.

I reluctantly lowered myself into the river again heading downstream, feeling so weak that it was hard to drag my legs along. After about fifteen minutes I pulled myself out and rested for ten minutes with my body suffering violent spasms from the intense cold. I had to force myself to get up and move.

The sun came out and, with it, the bite of the wind lessened a little, and some warmth came into the air, giving me a little more strength. I moved on along the bank feeling very exposed but unable to face getting back into the water and after a short while came to the main track and a destroyed bridge. I knew the line was close and this must be a sign of the German defensive perimeter. I crossed the fast flowing river and pulled my soaked body up the bank on which I hoped was now no-man's land.

I came to a cluster of houses and met an Italian and to my great relief he said, 'niente Tedesche qui' which I interpreted to mean there were no Germans here. He asked me into his house and offered me some wine. He beckoned that I should strip my outer clothes off and dry them in front of the fire while talking away at a speed I found impossible to follow. As my clothes dried and the warmth of the fire seeped into my limbs, I found myself drifting to sleep. I guess an hour or so passed before he nudged me awake and said I should go, pointing east to where the Allies were.

I was tantalizingly close to making it through, and so long as a German sniper didn't take a shot at me my chances were good. As I left the kind Italian's house I looked back at the snow-covered ridges and peaks of the Majella and reflected for a moment on Peter's whereabouts and how the Perseo family was coping. For a time I stood and willed Peter to be with me, hoping he may have followed my trail over the mountains. I suspected that he had given up but didn't want to dwell on this possibility as it was just too painful.

Turning away, I waved a goodbye to my new Italian friend and in my still damp and filthy clothes walked with confidence towards what I hoped was freedom.

I moved carefully down a narrow scrubby track, mindful that if I was close to the British line and appeared suddenly I was likely to get shot by anyone on watch. It was quite silent walking through this brush, and I felt a little warmer for the first time in an age. I felt so weak now that it was more of a stagger than a walk and I was losing grip of reality. Suddenly there was a shout ahead of me in English but with what sounded like an Australian accent. 'Stop right there and raise your hands in the air.' English not German! This was it; I was through.

I was filled with elation as I stood my ground with my arms raised, swaying from exhaustion, and two slightly nervous looking squaddies and a corporal approached me with bayonets fixed to their rifles. Behind them a machine gun poked out from a wall of sandbags. I must have looked a sight, a two-month-old beard, gaunt, filthy and probably smelling foul even after my semi-immersion in the river. I certainly didn't look a threat.

The corporal stood in front of me, rifle poised, with finger curled onto the trigger, and he asked me who I was. It took me a little time to remember, such was my exhaustion. I managed to bring some authority into my bearing, drawing myself a bit straighter and with the remaining energy in my body told him I was Captain Anthony Hough, 1 Special Air Service, escaped from Chieti PoW camp in September. His finger moved away from the trigger and his eyes softened, then brightened as he rather cheekily told me that I had taken quite some time to get through. With this he brought his men to attention and they gave me a respectful salute and welcomed me back.

He led me past the sandbag fortress with its occupants staring at me with awe, and onwards down the track for about three hundred yards where we reached a field tent and some officers and clerks. He handed me over to a captain and I learnt they were not Australians but the New Zealand Brigade Gino had mentioned. With the elation wearing off I was becoming very weak and he led me to an upturned log so I could sit while he organised transport. He produced a pack of cigarettes and gave me one, my first in a very long while which made me almost pass out after a few puffs, and handed me a steaming mug of sweet tea. A small truck of some sort arrived to take me to Brigade HQ in Casoli where I was able to have another delicious cup of tea and shave off my filthy, matted beard, the whole thing feeling quite unreal. An intelligence officer appeared and asked me a number searching questions about German dispositions in and around Pretoro which I answered as best I could. He was also interested in my route out and whether it was possible to infiltrate troops into the area from that direction. I said no unless it was a lightly armed force bent on a swift skirmish and retreat which would not really achieve much.

After a while I was moved further back to a Field Medical Centre sited in a large house some miles from Casoli and here I was put into a hot bath and was able to put on clean clothes before eating a small meal. After that I settled down on a camp bed fully clothed and with four blankets but still felt freezing.

Before my eyes closed, I reflected once more on what had happened to Peter, asking myself whether I should have insisted he stayed with me rather than go back into the valley. Maybe had I done so we would have been seen by the Germans, who knows. These thoughts didn't last long before I was gone into a dark peaceful place as deep as one could ever hope to experience.

Chapter 15

Freedom at last

I was awoken by an orderly gently shaking my shoulder and he offered me a large steaming mug of tea, the sun well up although hidden by a leaden sky and snow falling quite heavily. He left me to savour the tea and in this moment of privacy I was able to reflect on where I was and what I had achieved. It was hard to grasp that after a year of captivity and escape I had finally made it back. I was no longer threatened with the constant risk of discovery, the deprivation of living in the open without adequate food, cold and damp all the time, dependent on the goodwill of others. I had avoided recapture and made it back over challenging terrain and through the German line. What a feeling that was. After a while I was able to gather myself together and found on the chair in the room a neatly laid out uniform, a clean shirt, pants, socks and even a pair of boots that fitted. I could guess where my old clothes were!

When shaved and dressed in my smart clothes I found my way to the mess and had a breakfast of egg, bacon and large mug of piping hot tea. Goodness what bliss it was to eat hot food and have plenty of it. My surroundings felt surreal, as did no longer needing to be constantly alert to the chance of discovery. The mess was quiet at that time of day but occasionally a medical officer would wander in, coming over to me and offering a friendly shake of the hand accompanied by 'well done' with a pat on the shoulder. I felt well fed but the trials of the last few days and I suppose the last few months began to catch up with me and I felt the heaviness of total exhaustion.

An orderly asked if I would kindly follow him to meet with the major, and once that was done I would be moved further south. The major, of whom I had a hazy recollection from the day before, was an army doctor and wanted to have a chat about my condition, which he said was not good. I was suffering from jaundice; my skin was in a terrible condition and I was clearly very malnourished. I spoke about my repeated attacks of dysentery which he noted but said would probably clear after a few weeks of good food and rest. He also was interested to learn about my escape, so we talked for a while and he congratulated me before ushering me from his office, so he could get on with his day repairing broken bodies. He told me that the Canadians were involved in an attack to take Ortona on the coast, due east of where we were, and that it was pretty bloody with many killed and seriously injured. He had heard that morning that after eight days of intense fighting the town had finally been taken.

The PoW escapee processing was well organized, and after filling in a few forms, and eventually issued with identity documents, I was told to await a truck that would take me south-east to the town of Vasto, from where I would travel by train to Bari. My feet felt very tender and I felt colder than ever before even though I was now well dressed. That evening in Vasto there was an Entertainments National Service Association show put on for the troops which I enjoyed, although I felt strangely unmoved by the females parading around the stage. The whole thing seemed dreamlike and unreal, almost as if I was in some sort of fantasy world. The transition from the brutal experience crossing the mountains to a show in Vasto was surreal and I stared quite blankly at the stage, feeling a well of emotion that at some point would have to burst its banks. At the end of the show I was ushered away and taken to the station and boarded the train to Bari, an overnight journey.

On arrival the next morning on 30 December I was driven to accommodation in a large house commandeered for officers where I was offered a bath and put into a wonderfully comfortable bed, my first bed since 6 November! I still couldn't get warm enough and my feet were now quite swollen and there was no feeling in the tips of my fingers. I guess the fingers were numb as a result of using them to rub my legs during the night in the open and the feet were swollen from exposure to wet and mud all through that viciously cold night.

New Year's Eve 1943 was ushered in with a terrific party in an officers' mess nearby. I drank too much and found myself eating like a horse in an attempt to make up the two stone I had lost over the preceding months.

As I celebrated the coming of 1944 and all it had to offer, I began to relax properly for the first time, revelling in the companionship so freely shared.

I heard that the port of Bari had suffered a surprise night attack from the Luftwaffe earlier in December which had exacted a terrible toll. Over 1,000 lives were lost and many Allied merchant ships were sunk, including one carrying half a million gallons of high octane fuel. The destruction was awful and put things into perspective for me, having lived in my own little punctured bubble for several months.

After a few days of recovery, I moved by train to Taranto where I reflected on the last time I was there in such different circumstances, then dejected and uncertain about my future and now full of hope. The camp I was moved into was a very uncomfortable, cold stone building on the outskirts of the town centre, and with little to do I soon got bored. The next day I walked down to the officers' mess nearby for afternoon tea for want of anything else to do, but generally didn't like the place much and found myself getting quite irritated by the Italians.

On 6 January I finally got out of the dismal town. I was instructed to board a Paquebot called the *Ville d'Oran* headed for Philippeville in Algeria. The port was full of shipping, both naval vessels and freighters of all sizes. There was a great deal of activity on the wharves with cranes lifting freight off boats and soldiers embarking and disembarking. When I had negotiated my way through this throng and climbed up the gangplank to arrive on board I found I was in the company of about one thousand German prisoners who had been captured at the battle for Ortona. I sympathised with them but noticed the difference between the way we treated them and the way our Italian captors had treated us. Their officers were invited into our officers' mess and I found them to be courteous and pleasant to chat with. It made me even more aware of the stupidity of the conflict.

The captain told us that the boat was top heavy and in rough water it could take on a 30 degree roll, and during his last voyage he had had to lie flat on the deck to avoid going overboard which I found quietly amusing as he was very tubby. There was a French party on board who all became very sick on the journey to Syracuse even though there was only the weakest of swells. Syracuse, on the east coast of Sicily, was where we picked up many Americans returning to the USA after their successful capture of the island a few months earlier. The ship was bursting at the seams with men, so I hoped that we didn't encounter foul weather and put the dreaded roll to the test.

After an uncomfortable night crammed into a small cabin with three fellow officers, I got up early to watch the sun rise and was rewarded by a most special sight. Three battleships and two aircraft carriers escorted by eight destroyers passed on our port side heading in the direction of Taranto. The destroyers were charging around throwing up impressive bow waves, no doubt searching for enemy submarines. It was a sight to raise the spirits of all who witnessed it and caused much animated chat well into the day.

As I leaned on the rail of the ship gazing at the receding sight of these magnificent ships of war, I took time to reflect on my journey from Chieti into Pretoro and the surrounding hills, and my trek out. The first close call when the Germans got the wrong house having been informed of our presence by a fascist informer. The time the German officer came into the Perseo house and for reasons only known to him, his deciding not to inspect the top floor. The German troopers checking the cave as I lay hidden in a dark recess, and the two soldiers I almost walked straight into during my final bid for freedom. Such close encounters, any of which could have led to my capture.

Then the people themselves, Gino, the Santurbanos and their gorgeous niece Juliana, Armando, Angela Perseo and her large family; all of them courageous and generous. If it were possible, I decided I would make my way back to the village after the war to thank them for all they did. I gave a last thought to Peter, my companion and dear friend. It was unfortunate the snow had fallen so heavily after he left me as climbing back to the cave would have been treacherous. He could even then have still been hiding back in the valley, or better still having another go at escape. I had no news of him, nor did I expect to hear. I mused that it was more probable that he had been recaptured.

On the afternoon of 8 January we arrived in Philippeville and were able to enjoy much warmer late afternoon weather. We were told we would have to spend another night aboard, although the German prisoners were herded off the boat into waiting trucks which gave us all some breathing space.

I moved into a transit camp the next morning, but the conditions were so bad that I left immediately to live in the officers' club in town. It was here that I encountered the SAS again and was invited to lunch in their mess. This was repeated the next day when I met their colonel who invited me to dinner that evening. After a fine meal and probably too much good wine, we moved on to a nearby bar and the evening descended into chaos when some Canadians and Americans arrived looking for a fight. They weren't disappointed!

I awoke the next morning in the mess without any idea how I had got back. I had a raging temperature and was suffering bouts of rigors. I felt dreadful and my legs were both stiff and very painful. With my fever running high and with some effort I was able to get back to the officers' club where I went straight to bed. A medical orderly came to see me and I was immediately dispatched to the hospital with a telling off for behaving stupidly given my very poor condition. I became bedridden as my legs seemed to have packed up completely and the fever continued with a vengeance. The MO told me that I was going to be shipped by hospital train to Algiers the next night. I wasn't too ill to notice that the night sister was a very attractive woman and rather wished I was staying a while longer.

The following night two orderlies carted me off on a stretcher to board the night train to Algiers and we rattled along throughout the night eventually arriving in Algiers at 09:30 on 13 January where I was moved into the 96th military hospital.

Thankfully the fever began to ease and the acute pain in my legs lessened, so I felt pretty sure I wouldn't have to stay there for long. Hospital life really didn't suit me at all, being awoken at 06:00 for a wash before breakfast at 07:30. It didn't appear that anyone in the ward was terribly ill. I had a pleasant girl looking after me although she was a bit too fond of scolding me for trivial things.

After two days I was able to get up and wander around the grounds of the hospital and get some sun, but again fell foul of the Sister for being in my pyjamas outside. What a change from just a couple of weeks ago when life hung in the balance. I suppose I shouldn't complain as the nurses had my best interests at heart. My problem was that the jaundice was proving hard to shift and the attacks of dysentery were continuing. Some days I would feel okay and other days pretty sick. Even with the warmth of the Algerian sun I felt cold most of the time.

Life then ambled on for a week or so in the hospital. I underwent a succession of medical checks and, more disturbingly, psychological assessments. I was told it would be several months before I could even be considered for active duty. I was to return to the UK when a berth came available, probably on a naval ship. In the meantime I was to be confined to the hospital for another few weeks due to the jaundice and malnutrition. It wasn't until late January that I heard I could go back to England on a destroyer. I felt utter joy at the thought of heading home after nearly four years away.

I forget the name of the destroyer that took me home and that of the Medical Officer who looked after me so well. He became quite concerned at my condition and suggested I get to a hospital once back in England to undergo proper tests. We charged along at nearly maximum speed as the ship had urgent duties to perform in the Atlantic after reaching the UK. I hadn't much to do other than walk the deck and chat. I found a spot on the bow where I could lie gazing at the water rushing beneath me, feeling the pitch of the bow as it brushed waves aside during its headlong rush past Gibraltar and then north, forging onwards towards home and a bit of peace from all this noise. I found myself thinking of good friends and soldiers who had lost their lives during the great battles we fought, and it made me terribly sad that their lives had been squandered so.

On arrival at Plymouth on 8 February, I bade farewell to my new-found friends, boarded a train and headed into London, then onwards to Nottinghamshire where I reported to Rifle Brigade HQ at Ranby Camp in Retford, Nottinghamshire. Not much went on for the next few months, filling in here and there and kicking my heels. Problem was I wasn't too well at the time and kept having quite serious relapses of dysentery. Eventually it got so bad I was admitted into the Lincoln Military Hospital where I spent a month of acute boredom. The good news was I had learnt from the battalion commander that my escape had resulted in my being Mentioned in Despatches.

In July, feeling considerably better than I had done over the last six months, I was discharged from hospital to duty but was told to take extended leave. I journeyed south to London where I stayed overnight before taking an early train to Chipping Ongar in Essex, being met there by my father, tears in his eyes, and most unusually he hugged me tightly before leading me to the carriage that would take us the mile or so to Folyats. And there it was. The great house I left four years ago, its lawns dappled with dew, its woods standing aloof from the torment of the great conflict and its tranquillity bringing with it the first faltering step towards the peace of mind I desperately craved. If only my dear mother had been here to greet me.

And this is where my story ends.

Chapter 16

What happened next

On returning to the UK, my father was able to learn more about the fate of the other members of the SAS raiding party so fatefully engaged in late 1942.

Major Vivien Street reached his operating area and attacked a column on the road. The next day his section was chased and had to abandon their jeeps. They marched a considerable distance on foot but were eventually captured. He had the most remarkable escape from a submarine that was depth charged by a British plane operating out of Malta, surfaced and was eventually sunk by a British destroyer, but not before he and other prisoners were let out of their cramped compartment and they had dived overboard. A number perished but he was saved by an American pilot who had been a life saver in California before the war and they were picked up by the attacking destroyer.

He was greatly saddened to hear that Pat Hore-Ruthven had been killed during the raid. He had journeyed to his operational area with Vivien Street and together they blew up about twenty trucks filled with oil and petrol before mining the road and destroying telegraph poles. They then split up with Hore-Ruthven heading to his stretch of road near Misrata. There are varying accounts of what happened, but the most authentic is told by Sergeant Seekings who was with him. There were five of them in two jeeps and they attacked a well defended group of six trucks and three tanks. In the ensuing firefight Hore-Ruthven was hit in his right arm. Seekings managed to hurl a couple of grenades at the enemy dugouts and got Hore-Ruthven to a sandhill about fifty yards away. He couldn't move and told Seekings to get himself away, which he did. It appears that he then tried to run for it and got shot several times. He was taken to the Italian Military Hospital in Misrata but died soon after of his wounds. It seems there was another possible outcome to this tragedy, one that might have saved Hore-Ruthven's life.

Morris-Keating had a fight with Italian armoured cars in which he was wounded. He and his section were captured and I assume he spent the rest of the war as a PoW.

Maloney was suffering the whole time with a poisoned arm and was ambushed and captured before reaching his operational area. I assume he too spent the rest of the war as a PoW.

Carol Mather was spotted while crossing the main road and was chased from then onwards. He had a battle with Italians all the next day and was eventually captured. He successfully escaped from his northern PoW camp, trekking the length of the Apennines to do so. He became Montgomery's adjutant and writes amusingly about his experiences in his book *When the Grass Stopped Growing*. He refers to my father as Andy Hough rather than Anthony.

Nothing was known about one of the Free French members or Gallagher, although my father assumed the latter had got back to the supply trucks.

Alston, Thesiger and David Martin, the other Free French member, fared better as they were near the dump at El Fascia and therefore able to return after a raid to replenish supplies. Over four raids they had inflicted considerable damage on road traffic and were eventually instructed to rendezvous with Stirling at Bir Guedaffia in early January.

As to his own section, the diversion he set up to give his men a chance of escape didn't work as the Italians had completely surrounded their position. All five of them were captured without injury and sent to Italy as PoWs. They met Vivien Street at the PoW camp in Tripoli and told Street they feared my father had been killed.

The raid was partly successful as a fair amount of damage was done both to transport and morale. The Italians had thought they were safe from attack this far behind the front line and it was a rude awakening for them to discover otherwise. These wraiths of the night would descend on them bringing death and destruction and hampering the supply to Rommel's army. It did achieve its objective of forcing more movement during the day which made the convoys susceptible to air attack. Thirty brave and highly trained men were effectively discarded by Stirling, and whether this was a good use of them is debatable. It was the worst loss to date of SAS men on a raid and Stirling tried to lay the blame on the general lack of experience of B Squadron. This doesn't wash though and is a poor excuse for a failure to anticipate the difficulty faced from operating so far behind enemy lines in an area filled to the brim with enemy troops. The B Squadron mission was reckless and while it had achieved good results in bringing disruption to the enemy supply line the men involved never really had much chance of escape. What they did achieve was to carry out their mission to the best of their ability and without hesitation under gruelling conditions, displaying all the best characteristics of the SAS.

On 22 December 1944 my father was posted to Europe to join 21 Army Group, part of which was his old brigade. He was actively involved in the campaign to drive the Germans deeper and deeper into their own territory. After the war ended in May 1945, he was posted as an assistant Town Major in Springe, Germany, which lies south-west of Hanover. A town major's role is the running of an occupied town, similar in some ways to what a mayor would do. A mayor in both France and Germany has a much more powerful role than in the UK, or certainly did at that time. In November 1945 he moved down the road to Bad Pyrmont where he was Town Major until March 1946, when he was discharged from the regular army with the rank of major.

My father met my mother during his leave from late July to September 1944. They married in July 1946. My mother, Valerie Hennessy, was the daughter of Sir Patrick Hennessy, who had been knighted in 1942 for his services to aircraft production in Lord Beaverbrook's Ministry for Aircraft Production. My grandfather went on to become Chairman and Chief Executive of the Ford Motor Company in the UK. My mother had turned down an offer to read English at Cambridge in 1942, had joined the WRNS, and was posted to Bletchley as part of the Enigma decoding group. She could have taken her place at Cambridge after being released from active service but with marriage on the horizon decided on family life.

Peter Gunn, my father's good friend and travelling companion, was recaptured on his return to the valley on Christmas Day 1943 and spent the remainder of the war as a PoW in Germany. He spent a fair amount of time with my family after the war and became my godfather at my christening in July 1952. I was never to meet him, as soon after he lost contact with the family and my mother was vague about why. He lived near Peterborough, Cambridge, and died in 1986. I don't know whether my father kept in contact with him and it does seem odd that someone with whom he shared such times and whom he asked to be my godfather would quite suddenly lose contact. One of those many vagaries within our family where much was left unsaid.

The Artists Rifles had been disbanded in 1945 but was reformed in July 1947 and transferred to the Army Air Corps as the 21st Special Air Service Regiment (Artists) (Reserve). The number 21 was chosen to perpetuate two disbanded wartime regiments, 2 SAS and 1 SAS. After the Malaysian conflict, members of the regiment involved in that campaign formed 22 SAS, the only time a Territorial Army unit had been used to form a unit in the regular army.

My father joined 21 SAS (Artists) on 10 January 1950 and left on 26 May 1952. He spent the next forty years employed by the family paperboard business, always as a director and from 1970 as managing director. After his retirement from executive duties in 1990 he remained as chairman until his death in 2000. He became an excellent golfer, playing off a handicap of four and frequently able to play sub-par. He was a member of Thorndon Park Golf Club, becoming Captain in 1959 and President from 1993 till his death in 2000. He writes amusingly in a book celebrating the millennium: 'The club became my second home. My wife, fortunately long-suffering, disagrees with this and insists it has been my first home.' One of his great friends at the club was Charles Newman VC who led 2 Commando on the St Nazaire raid in March 1942. He was also a member of Aldeburgh Golf Club in Suffolk. He won many golfing prizes which included the Artists Rifles President's Cup on three occasions.

He had married well and lived comfortably, running a successful business through challenging times. He was a kind, courteous man who was easy to be around. He rarely spoke of the war, preferring to tuck that part of his life away and allow it to slumber in the background. He occasionally would demonstrate a few unarmed combat moves which thankfully I have never had to use. He had a number of friends living locally who had similar experiences during the war and when together the gates would open for a short while, usually after a good dinner and a great deal of alcohol.

I have a letter he wrote to my grandfather from the PoW camp at Bari in January 1943 and which is heavily redacted.

Campo PG.75 P.M.3450.

'Dear Daddy, I am in a camp in Italy with quite a lot of other fellows, and we have quite an amusing time……….. they fairly whistled me out of Africa straight to Italy – I must say its pleasant to be out of the desert at last, after nearly two years in it, and of course after desert life, PoW life is extremely restful and almost better, although I expect after a bit I shall begin to get too bored. They have various classes here, French, German etc. So I think I can keep myself amused. The food is fair………..

I hope the business is going well – Please give my regards to Bateman and Otley and the others of the staff and wish them a happy new year from me. Please also give my love to Granny and others, especially Stephen.

Well no more now, I shall be writing every week. My love to you, from Anthony. P.S. I was captured on December 20th.

My father's elder brother Robert had joined the Inns of Court HAC before the war and was commissioned into the Yorkshire Hussars at the outbreak of war, serving in North Africa and Europe before being demobbed with the rank of Major in 1945. His younger brother John was an interesting case. He was not naturally suited to warfare. He was a gentle, highly intelligent, artistic soul who went up to Magdalene College Cambridge after Uppingham, graduating in 1940. He joined the Leicester Yeomanry Territorial Army in October 1939 and was commissioned into the regular army in May 1941, and soon after joined the Queen's Bays. The regiment was posted to the Middle East in September 1941, arriving at the end of November. After a period of desert training the regiment was fully engaged against the Axis. He was wounded in his left arm in July 1942 and was sent to South Africa where there was the greatest chance of being able to repair nerve damage. After a series of operations he returned to the UK in February 1943. In August 1944 he was posted to Italy and was wounded in October of that year. Unfortunately it was the same arm as before and he was permanently disabled, therefore being discharged from the Army after a lengthy period in hospital. He was not a warrior and admitted after the war that he had been terrified by battle. However, he acquitted himself with distinction and in many respects was the bravest of them all.

What is surprising is that my paternal grandfather and two great uncles fought through the First World War, and my father and two uncles fought through the Second World War, and they survived, with only John suffering a permanent injury.

Like so many thousands, they gave all for their country without hesitation and without complaint. The extent to which they may have suffered trauma subsequently is unknown as they never, ever talked about their emotional selves, or at least not to us children. How different their generation was to today's needy society that thinks and talks so much about its emotional hang-ups.

Appendix 1

Opening the door to the past

A short while before my father died in 2000 my sister Alex discovered, tucked into the back of a tatty old file in his desk, a pencil-written account of an SAS operation in December 1942, his capture and subsequent escape from the Chieti prisoner of war camp in Eastern Italy in September 1943. She gave it to me after he died, and I had it typed up. It forms the basis of this story.

In late September 2017 I flew to Naples with two of my very good friends, David Brandler and Julian Winser, where I had organised a hire car for us to drive across Italy to the Adriatic coast, just south of Pescara in the province of Chieti.

The diary had included the name Gino Francioni and the first names of people living in the village of Pretoro in the Majella region of the Abruzzo, who had helped him during his escape. Pretoro is a village seemingly glued to a steep hill and typical of villages in that region of Italy.

I had booked for us to stay in a B&B called Casa Mila owned by a lady called Patrizia who spoke little English. With the help of translation software I wrote her an email explaining why I was coming to Pretoro and the first names of some of the people who had helped my father, in the hope that she might be able to assist me in tracking them down. She replied asking for a wartime photo of him which I sent and I heard no more. With the exception of Francioni my father had not noted the surnames of these people.

Our drive from Naples airport to Chieti took just over three hours, mostly alongside the mighty Abruzzo mountains rising steeply on our left with many villages and towns clinging to its lower slopes. Our purpose in Chieti was to visit the PoW camp my father was incarcerated in for six months and hopefully get to see the inside of the water tower he hid in during his escape. The camp had reverted to a military barracks after the war and is now occupied by the military police. Brian Lett has written a book called

An Extraordinary Italian Imprisonment which describes the camp during the time his father was a prisoner, and after contacting him he kindly offered to make an introduction to the camp colonel to try to arrange a visit. This was successful and we were told to report to the main gate at 10am on Monday 25 September 2017. The camp lies in Chieti Scalo which sits beneath the hilltop town of Chieti, about ten miles south of Pescara near the Adriatic coast.

We arrived in Chieti in time for a late lunch and a chance to walk around the city. Chieti is reputedly one of the most ancient cities in Italy, founded in 1181 BC, and due to its age was declared an open city in the Second World War and not bombed by either side. Its wide avenues are framed with gracious buildings and the cathedral tower rises grandly above all. It is built atop a steep hill and the area of level ground is small relative to the size of the city, which spills off the top into the valley below. Driving in Italy has its challenges at the best of times and driving up the hill into the centre is a challenge requiring a strong heart, as the local Italians know where they are going and do so at speed without much patience for those struggling to find their way.

The next morning, we left our B&B in good time for our 10am meeting at the camp, which was just as well as finding the barracks was not easy, made more difficult from taking the wrong road from the centre of town. We finally arrived at the designated time at an impressively tall and solid main gate and were ushered into the compound by two armed soldiers. Colonel Marcello Sciarappa was called and after a short wait he arrived, immaculately dressed and with a welcoming smile to greet us. He spoke fluent English having spent time in Canada and was charming, knowledgeable and enthusiastic about his role as temporary tour guide. He was especially interested in the story I had to tell about my father's incarceration and escape and spent a good deal of time walking us to various points in the camp where escape tunnels had been dug out. It surprised me how small the access points were and the distance the tunnels had to travel to get under the main wall. It would have been frightening toiling away underground in a very confined space, with little air to breathe and trying to ignore the constant risk of a roof collapse.

The camp is laid out as a rectangle about 350 metres long and 250 metres wide, accommodating an Italian section at the front containing a parade area, and administration and living blocks occupying about a third of the space. The surrounding wall is 4 metres high. There would have been a high wire fence separating the Italian area from the PoWs. Inside the prisoner area there had been four blocks and a cookhouse. Each block was divided into two and the camp housed about twelve hundred men after three hundred were transferred further north in May 1943. At the time of our visit the interior of the camp was enhanced by an avenue of mature fir trees and many of the same growing within the walls, often nestling close to the blocks.

He led us further into the camp until we finally arrived at the water tower, standing tall at the far right-hand corner and rising about twenty metres. We pushed open a metal door and there we were, standing inside an open area rising to a ceiling high above us and iron steps leading up the left wall to a small hatch giving access to the loft bearing the water tank. It seemed as if the middle floor where they had hidden had been removed. I had already been able to picture life in the camp from reading Brian Lett's book and seeing the unchanged buildings brought it all to life. Now I was standing, mouth slightly agape, looking up and picturing Dad with three others desperately trying to avoid making a noise for fear of discovery. It would have been hot, uncomfortable and acutely dangerous but they sat it out for long enough for the Germans to clear the camp of the thousand or so prisoners and then clear off themselves. What a moment this was for me to be able to stand here and think of him as a young, determined man, willing enough to have a go.

We wandered slowly back to the main gate chatting about what the camp was used for now and generally savouring the moment. I had brought a new copy of Brian Lett's book which I gave to the Colonel as a small parting gift to thank him. He waved us away and the tall metal gates were shut gently behind us by the two well-armed guards.

We left Chieti and drove south-west for forty kilometres, visiting a few of the mountainside villages and getting a feel for the terrain before turning back and climbing towards Pretoro. One of the villages was Pennapiedimonte, which features in the story and was the western edge of the German line, as the terrain was impassable further west. A deep gorge runs from the Majella to the west of Pennapiedimonte and appeared to be treacherous. The grand mountains of the Majella reared up to the north and west creating a daunting backdrop to the village. Pennapiedimonte itself hangs on the edge of a steep slope with terraces looking south and west. The tourist season had finished in early September and the village appeared devoid of life; even a small café on the west facing terrace was closed.

We climbed back into the car and drove onto the main road taking us east towards Pretoro. The road was almost empty of traffic, constantly rising and falling as it wound its way in and out of the valleys. The temperature was a pleasant twenty degrees with light cloud drifting gently above us, but the mountains were shrouded in a heavy mist which spilled down their vertiginous sides, with tendrils reaching for the valley below.

After a while meandering through tiny roadside villages, we saw the sign to Pretoro and climbed steeply to reach the town's lower limits which lay a few hundred feet below the upper part. The road zig-zagged through unkempt houses until reaching a turning left which would take us towards the church and which I felt was always a good target if uncertain of the direction one should take. After another two sharp bends we came to a smaller road to our left, almost single track, running alongside the church and this we took. We drove down this narrow road passing between tall, gloomy buildings and then burst into a most charming small piazza, where we were able to park the car. The piazza has a magnificent view over the surrounding hills towards Rapino and further still one can see the sea. To our right we found Casa Mila B&B, its stout wooden door firmly shut and locked but with a sign saying to ring the bell of the house opposite on the other side of the piazza. Outside the door bordering the protective rails was a small table and chairs sitting under a wooden arbour and at the back of the piazza was a grocery store.

After stretching our legs and enjoying the marvellous view we rang the doorbell as directed and a short, elderly woman came out who spoke almost no English. David was able to explain in his basic Italian that we were staying in the B&B. Having identified me as the son of Anthony Hough she spoke at length. We were unable to understand most of it, but it sounded hopeful. She left us to call Patrizia, who arrived a little later and ushered us into the B&B. The ground floor is a reception area off which there are two bedrooms. Upstairs where we were directed are three more bedrooms, two doubles and a single, and here we dumped our stuff. Above this is a further eaves bedroom. My room was a double, looking out over the same view as the piazza, with a precipitous drop from a Juliet balcony onto a narrow alley between Casa Mila and the house below.

David spoke rudimentary Italian, having for many years sold leather into Italy. When he struggled with comprehension or getting himself understood he had mastered arm and shoulder movements that seemed to get the message conveyed. Patrizia explained in halting English and rapid Italian that her father Verino Perseo lived across the piazza and Maria, the lady we had met earlier, was her mother. Verino's sister Maria lived further up the hill and they both would like to meet us the next morning at Verino's house. Patricia explained that the Perseo family had bought the Casa Mila from Gino Francioni after the war and that her father Verino and aunt, Maria, remembered my father. I realised that I had hit the jackpot and was staying in the very house my father first stayed in when reaching Pretoro, maybe even sleeping in the same bedroom.

After dining in a local taverna and playing a few rounds of prediction whist while sampling the robust locally produced wine my father talked about, we took a walk along the cobbled streets of Pretoro, up and down endless stone steps framed by houses with solid wooden doors and along the narrow, dimly lit passageways. From the top of the village to its bottom there must be a drop of 100 metres. The bright moon illuminated the valley rising steeply away to the west and the gentle breeze caressed the branches of the trees carpeting the slope. The village was so silent it felt as if we were the only people there. Occasionally a dog would bark excitedly at our passing; otherwise we met no-one. I could visualise how the narrow alleys would have appeared in 1943 with no electric lighting to guide our feet.

Feeling refreshed we headed back to the B&B and bed, filled with excited anticipation at the meeting tomorrow.

Breakfast the next morning was had in the basement and to get there we were asked to go outside and walk to the left of the house and down steps to another entrance. It is possible to get from the reception area down stone stairs but it leads through the kitchen, so this is used only if the weather is bad. These were the steep steps my father referred to when making his escape from the village.

Shortly before 10am the next morning I stood outside the solid wooden door of Casa Mila in bright sunlight looking out over the railings at the fabulous view over the hills to the sea far in the distance. I heard a screech of tyres and the sound of an engine protesting its abuse. I turned to see an ancient Fiat Panda charge out of the narrow road into the piazza and onwards to the only remaining parking space available in the small piazza. Out climbed a smartly dressed, short, slender, aged woman, and after giving the door a good slam, enough to rock the car on its remaining springs, she disappeared back down the lane. I was later introduced to her as Maria Perseo, the sister of Verino and the 11-year-old courier of food and wine to my father in 1943.

Shortly after David and Patrizia joined me and we went over to the Perseo house, the entrance of which was just along the road leading back to the church. Patrizia rang the bell before letting us in and ushered us upstairs to the living room where we met Verino and Maria for the first time. Verino stood about 1.7 metres tall with a shock of white hair and powerful broad shoulders. He greeted us with a wide smile and a firm handshake. His sister Maria was a sprightly, slim attractive lady with a vivacious personality and a great deal of energy, having already displayed a fair amount of it dealing with her car. It was hard to believe that she was 85 years old and her brother 87. They made us feel welcome and relaxed, sat us down at the dining table and offered us coffee and treats to eat. Verino's wife Maria, whom we had met the afternoon before, scurried in from the kitchen laden with pastries and the coffee. She too welcomed us into her home and made sure we had everything we needed. We were joined by a young lady called Angela D'Angelo who had recently taught Italian students English in Glasgow and was there to translate.

At first Angela struggled to find enough of a gap in the animated conversation from Verino and Maria to translate into English, but when eventually they drew breath I learnt that my father and Peter were well remembered and our arrival at the village had triggered memories of their youth during the German occupation. They spoke of Dad resolutely wearing his uniform even though it was threadbare in places and of how tall he was. The conversation rapidly leapt out of the house into the cave where they hid for several weeks and the excitement the children felt carrying food to them under the noses of the Germans. The house we were in had been substantially rebuilt by Verino with little resemblance to how it was back in 1943.

Assunta, Elina and Salvatore, the other three children mentioned in the story, had died and the tragedy in their eyes was that it had taken me so long to find my way to their village. We then had the most wonderful conversation with both Verino and Maria talking animatedly about the war and my father and his friend Peter Gunn. They said that they had no idea my father had survived and because they had not heard from him had presumed he had died while making his final break for freedom.

They asked why he had never contacted them after the war, I expect not least to thank them for risking their lives to shelter him. I found this a very difficult one to answer and explained that in the '50s and '60s travel anywhere other than some main cities was not easy and very expensive. After that, time had moved on and I expect he hadn't wanted to dwell on this period in his life.

Maria was animated, happy, tearful and above all incredibly thankful that I had come to the village. In turn I was greatly affected by the moment and found it to be one of the most unique experiences of my life. I thanked them for what they had done and the sacrifices they had made. They told me that I was the first person to come to Pretoro on behalf of the PoWs that sought shelter in the village.

I then spent the next hour or so reading extracts from the story of his time in Pretoro and his eventual escape. We spoke about the families that had sheltered him before the Perseo family took him in and they acknowledged the names of the people involved. They were especially interested in the route he took out over the mountains and commented on how dangerous it was in mid-winter with snow and ice on the ground. A number of villagers had lost their lives over the years slipping on ice and falling hundreds of metres into the valley below.

Pretoro people are famed for their woodwork and Verino had built a successful joinery business making, amongst other things, doors and wooden staircases which he sold all over Europe, employing fifty people in the village. His daughters Patrizia and Angela had worked with him in the factory helping to run the business but eventually the entry of eastern European nations into the EC had allowed the free flow of lower priced products into the market causing his business to close. The large factory stands today occupying several acres of land below the village, big enough to receive trees which would be cut into planks before being tooled into product, a now silent testament to his determination to build something from almost nothing. The photo of him as a young man, hanging just inside the entrance to Casa Mila, gives one a good idea of the strength of his character.

After this long and animated discussion Verino asked if we would meet with the Mayor, Sabrina Simone Sindaco, who was very interested in our visit to the village. Accompanied by Verino we walked down to the church, then to its right where steps cut the way between houses to the road below. Along this road we found the civic offices which was where the mayor worked, and she was there to greet us. Sabrina Simone was an attractive, vivacious woman to whom Julian took an instant shine. She was most keen for a summarised account of my father's time in Pretoro and the story of his escape to be translated into Italian so she could use it as part of the village's promotional literature. I agreed to let Angela have a copy in English and she was tasked with the translation.

Verino said that the next morning he and Maria would walk into the valley with us and show us the cave my father hid in as well as other caves that were used by the villagers. At that point he bade us farewell and walked back up the steps without any apparent difficulty.

We walked again to the top of the village to see if we could find some-where to eat lunch and in passing I noticed a very old man in his workshop standing on a large pile of sawdust. I beckoned the others and went in to discover a room where the floors and walls were covered with large scale replicas of ancient buildings of Italy, all carved with loving precision and skill. There were other things of interest such as a helicopter and a blunderbuss. He spoke only Italian and was proud of his work although made no attempt to sell any of it. The replicas were large and the detail intricate making me wonder where one could place them even if he was prepared to sell. We heard later that he made these models for pleasure and wasn't interested in selling.

We couldn't find a place to eat so descended back to the piazza and bought cheese, bread and dried meats from the small grocery store and sat outside Casa Mila enjoying the food and the wonderful view. I had a good walking map of the area which we studied intently to decide our afternoon hike into the hills which would give us our first feel for the terrain.

Having finished lunch, Julian, David and I drove high up the valley until we came to an access point for the walk we had decided on leading us into the mountains and the Col D'Angelo. We set off under a brooding sky walking through dense forest carpeting the steep mountainside. As we walked, we had to be careful not to step on Apennine or Fire salamanders with their deep yellow spots, that were in abundance along the pathway. It brought into sharp focus my father's comment on these amphibians when making his final bid for freedom.

We walked for many miles down into the valley, sometimes struggling to find our way, but somehow got to the right junctions, even if it meant forcing our way through dense undergrowth. It was comforting to know that Julian, who had flown night sorties in the Army Air Corp, was able to find his way! While the valley ran all the way down to Pretoro we came to a small plateau and here we turned to complete the loop, which required an arduous climb in now foul weather, and which seemed to go on for an eternity. On the way up we came across a large cave complex called the Grotta dell'Eremita (hermit's cave) which after the evacuation of the village in December 1943 was home to 100 villagers. The cave cut deeply into the mountain above with a ceiling tall enough for me to stand upright. Storage holes had been cut into its walls and there were rings of rocks where one could imagine fires burning all day through the bitterly cold winter. It wasn't an easy place to get to so would have afforded the villagers a degree of security. The gloom of the afternoon grew deeper and the cold rain fell harder so we cut short our exploring and hurried back on to the steep track. After a further half hour, we reached the junction with the path we had taken earlier which was then only a short walk to the car. As darkness was falling, we arrived back at Casa Mila soaked to the skin but happy that even with our advancing years we could still endure a rugged trek without complaint.

Glorious sunshine and a deep blue sky greeted my awakening the next morning. Gentle cool air pushed aside the light net curtain and brought a clean freshness to the air in the room. The view from the small side window was up the deeply forested valley rising steeply to the mountains beyond. I dressed and went down into the basement where breakfast had been laid by Patrizia. Cereal, fruit and bread and a delightful sweet cake which I wrapped to eat later that morning. After breakfast we made ready for our excursion into the valley.

Maria announced her arrival with the grinding of gears as she rocketed down the road into the piazza and managed to halt with a screech of brakes, just stopping before the iron railings protecting a sheer fall into the alley below. Verino wandered out of his house and said we would drive the short distance down the hill to a terrace at the edge of the village facing the valley. The large terrace was big enough for many cars and I assumed during the summer months it was a parking area for hikers. There was an overgrown track on its edge which led steeply down through trees and with Verino leading the way we pushed our way through and down loose rock steps to find it broadened out somewhat into an earth and scree track. I was concerned at its steepness on account of Verino's age, but he showed not the slightest hesitation, striding out with good balance. Maria had the agility of someone many years younger and launched herself onto the path with carefree determination carrying a long staff to give occasional support.

A short way down and closer than I had expected, Verino stopped and started to pull away some of the vegetation running alongside the path. After a while exploring a short stretch, he discovered what he was looking for, a narrow, overgrown path leading slightly uphill at an angle to the village above. We walked carefully along the rocky track, the slope to our right falling sharply down to the river, until we came across a cave set deeply into the face of the cliff about thirty metres below the lower village. It was shrouded in hanging vegetation and invisible from the main path to the river. Its proximity to the village would have made me nervous of discovery, but it was very well concealed. The cave was in two parts with an opening in the shape of an arch joining the two. It had a soft bed of leaves underfoot and a roof of about 1.7 metres. It faced towards the rising valley and was well protected from northerly and easterly winds. This was my father's and Peter's home for a month, and in November it would have been cold and damp. What a moment this was. I tried without much success to imagine how life would have been, waiting each day for one of the eager children to bring food and news of life in the village, the long hours of boredom in the damp and cold of the cave, the constant anxiety of capture and the difficulty of dealing with daily ablutions. It would have been very tough, day after long day, night after long night.

Verino and Maria then led us down to the river, a further drop of about fifty metres, then following the river upstream a short way to show us a now disused flour mill, set into a deep twin-storey cave excavated out of the rock. Water from the river would have been diverted to drive the grinding wheel. It would appear that escapees spent time in this cave as the date of 1943 was carved into the rock accompanied by a ghoulish face and the initials MA. The river in 1943 was much more abundant than now as the diverting of water to feed the cities of Pescara and Ortona had yet to happen.

They also showed us other caves used initially by the villagers after the village was evacuated in December 1943, and before they moved more deeply into the mountains. As we walked further up the track we came to a steep cliff to our right which looked as if it had been mined for rock. It rose about 300 metres vertically with trees lining its summit.

This was as far as Verino and Maria wanted to go, so we turned and retraced our steps following the river until we came to the steep track leading back to the village. It was here that I half expected Verino and Maria to show some signs of age, but they would have none of it! They led us back up the slippery and steep slope to the terrace with vigour and sure-footedness. Such vitality for two octogenarians!

After our walk Patrizia said that we were invited to dinner at her father's house that evening where we would meet her husband Mario and her sister Angela.

Bidding our temporary farewells we decided to do some exploring of the region and drove over the mountain lying above Pretoro, passing the Marcantonio ski resort on the way, and on down to a spa town called Caramanico Terme, sitting above a gorge cut by the Orfento river, which I had read was a fabulous walk. After lunching on delightful pasta dishes in a small taverna near the entrance to the gorge, we strolled down a steep track to find the river carving its way through tree-lined rocky terrain with crystal clear water tumbling into rock pools before swirling and gurgling its way down the valley.

The sun, filtered by the trees, cast a soft glow over the gorge creating an immensely peaceful place to walk. It was quite beautiful and sometimes the sheer rock walls stretching up from the river would cast deep shadows over the path bringing with it a mystical atmosphere. The path wound its way alongside the river and when blocked by a boulder or the steepness of the cliff a wooden footbridge would carry us to the other bank, the water tumbling energetically underneath and swirling into deep rock pools.

Some of these footbridges were supported by massive boulders lying in the middle of the river. The contrast of colours made the walk immensely peaceful, yellowy rust-coloured rock coated in vivid lichen, tangled ivy hanging over ledges, many shades of green in the tree-filled slopes on either side and multicoloured pebble shallows on the inside bank of the meander.

After half an hour we came to a path that led steeply up to a road that ran across a bridge over the gorge and back to the town. Julian and David decided to take the road, but I had another agenda and elected to return by way of the gorge, ostensibly to enjoy the beauty of it all once again. My real reason was that near one of the footbridges I had spied an invitingly deep rock pool and had decided to have a swim. When I got there, I stripped off my clothes and plunged into the freezing water hoping that I wouldn't be discovered by a group of walkers. It was both refreshing and quite ethereal.

We drove back over the mountain to Pretoro in time to wash and change for our dinner with the Perseo family. Patrizia met us in the reception area of Casa Mila and she said to me that I was now considered to be one of their family, something that took me by surprise and made me feel that the visit had a greater impact than I would have thought possible. I shall cherish that moment for the rest of my life.

We were made very welcome by this charming, happy family, with local wine flowing and endless trays of food appearing from the kitchen on which were delightful dishes of pasta, pastries and meat. There were three generations of Perseo at the dinner, and while comprehension proved a challenge, we had a marvellous time. Patrizia introduced me to her husband Mario, a tall, good-looking man who was by all accounts an excellent skier and an experienced mountain guide. I said to Maria that after seventy-four years she was still feeding a Hough, and she replied that it was a pleasure then, albeit filled with risk, and a great pleasure now. Filled to the brim with food and wine and feeling ebullient from it we said our farewells and took a fast paced final tour of the village in a fairly unsuccessful attempt to walk it off.

The next day brought an end to this extraordinary journey into the past and we said our sad goodbyes to these wonderful, resolute and independent hillside villagers. Pretoro is a village of great character situated within the stunning Majella National Park, an area of outstanding beauty in a part of Italy that is relatively unknown.

We packed the car with the few pieces of luggage we carried and waved our goodbyes, promising to return. By now the whole village was aware of us and why we were there and there were quite a few in the piazza to see us off. Later in this book I will tell the story of how these brave and resourceful villagers survived being thrown out of their homes to live in the mountains in the middle of winter. It is an extraordinary tale.

We drove back to Naples reflecting with joy at how well the three days had gone and how much we had learnt. We had an overnight stay in Naples with an early flight home the next day and it had been left to David to book our accommodation. Unfortunately he had got muddled with the hotel name and had booked us into an awful hotel suffering trains, planes and traffic, but that is another story!

Having returned to the UK, my plan to go back to the village in winter to better experience the hardship of life there was thwarted by my mother's declining health and her death in February 2018. After many months sorting out her affairs, I was able to make plans for another trip in early September 2018 and this time I intended to stay for a couple of weeks to give me time to explore village life and to find Dad's route out when he made his final bid for freedom.

I arrived back in Pretoro late evening on 5 September 2018. The village was quiet and Casa Mila empty save David Brandler and me. David was accompanying me for five days on this trip and my cousin James Hough was due to join me after ten days. For the next few days we walked deep into the mountains, most of the time walking under beech and fir, dropping easily down steep tracks onto the valley floor then climbing slowly back up the 1,000 or so metres to reach the ridge we had left several hours before. The terrain here is very steep and carpeted in dense forest up to about 2,000 metres so much of the time is spent under the canopy without much visual relief from endless trees. Occasionally we would spy deer and boar but birds seemed to have left the area as very little birdsong was heard.

It was now that Patrizia told me that her husband Mario, who I had met the year before, had died very tragically in the mountains. It was late November and early snows had fallen. He had hiked up with skis and had slipped on ice, plunging over a sheer drop. This brought into stark reality just how dangerous these mountains are in winter.

It wasn't until 15 September that I was able to organise a more formal meeting with Verino and Maria, although we had chatted together a number of times before. I wanted to find out about life in the village before and during the war and dig a little deeper into the characters of their family.

Firstly, we spoke about their mother, Angela Perseo, and what kind of woman she was. Strict, came the answer, very hardworking as she had to be as her husband died in 1934 falling from a horse in the lower valley while working the fields. Her husband Domenico had spent much of his time in the USA doing what no-one seems to know and returned from time to time. He sent money home, enough to support the family.

Angela had a grocery store on the ground floor of her house sitting on the Piazza Roma. Much of the produce for sale was grown and produced by the family, olives, tomatoes, potatoes, eggs, milk and grapes for wine making, with salt, pasta, sugar and tobacco bought in Chieti. While there was a bus that ran from Pretoro to Chieti the journey to collect supplies was by horse and cart. Wheat was also grown locally, and bread was made by the family for daily sale. There were wheat mills by the river to grind the wheat into flour. Rabbits were bred in captivity and killed for meat. The family had cows, sheep, chickens, pigs and goats. In the autumn work would begin preparing foods for the winter, drying meat, preserving fruit and storing flour. Wine was also made locally with enough stored to last the year. At that time the river was much more abundant and irrigation channels were taken from it. Nowadays the regional government has installed many diversions to supply water to Pescara and the flow is much diminished, especially in the summer months. This is true of most water flow from the mountains.

Villagers worked their own plots of land and there was produce trade between them.

There was no water piped up into the village and it had to be collected from the valley for use in the houses. Most washing, both personal and clothes, took place at the river. At the beginning of the war electricity was supplied to the village for only about two hours each day by a small company in Fara Filiorum, but there was limited use of it as internal and external wiring was very basic. Lighting was mostly provided by candles or oil lamps. The steep and narrow streets were not lit and in deepest winter hand-held wooden stakes with flaming pitch were used to light the way through the streets. There was no fear of the dark and moving at night without torches was not considered a problem.

The villagers had a reputation for wood craftsmanship and much varied woodwork was produced, including weaving of baskets. This was sold throughout the region and as far afield as Rome. Wood was also cut and sold for firewood as there was an abundant supply in the hills.

As there was no running water in the village, hygiene was limited. Often the toilet would be in the straw on which the animals lived, usually in the cellar of the house. Chamber pots were used in the house at night and emptied into the valley.

Angela had five children, Assunta being the eldest born in 1921. She was above average height for a girl in that region of Italy, slim, attractive and highly intelligent (as were all the Perseo children). By the outbreak of war she was nearing the end of her schooling in Chieti and it wasn't until after the war that she went to university in Rome. In her final year in 1940 she would board weekly at the Nun's Orsoline College in Chieti, getting there by bus. There was a daily bus running from Pretoro to Chieti, however the children preferred to board. There was a junior school in Pretoro teaching from five years to ten.

When Assunta finished her studies with distinction in 1941 Angela gave her the gift of a radio, which could be used each day during that two-hour electricity supply window. This was quite a novelty in the village and many came to listen to it. Later when the Germans came to the village an informer told them of the radio which by then was illegal and they came to the house to search for it. However, Assunta had been prewarned and hid it away. The Germans became quite aggressive but hadn't taken into account the strength of Angela, the mother, who with folded arms lambasted them. As a punishment they told Assunta she would be required to wash all the German vehicles in the piazza, quite a job given the difficulty of bringing water up. Angela helped her, and this tough, independent proud woman was furious with the Germans for their attitude and conceit.

Elina was born in 1925 and was a young woman by 1943. Again her studies were halted by the German encampment in the village. She had little option other to remain in the village and help Assunta run the home.

Salvatore was the fifth child born in 1934. He was vivacious like his sister Maria but slightly less part of the family. After the war he went to complete his studies in Rome and became a teacher. The family sold two pigs and gave one more to the college to pay for his advanced education.

Village life was hard enough anyway so didn't change much until September 1943 after the Italian surrender. Many of the young men had been conscripted into the war and would have fought in North Africa. The local cemetery has eighteen recorded deaths of villagers, some interestingly after September 1943, the date of the Italian surrender. A strong partisan movement formed in Italy at this time, although I was unable to see much sign of this in Pretoro.

The entrance to the Perseo house was different to today in that it came off the piazza through the grocery store, with stairs to the right. In the basement was an olive press and blindfolded donkeys were used to turn the stone press. Livestock was kept here in the winter on straw and there was a door to a narrow track on the side of the hill which led to the valley and was well shielded from the piazza by trees. This incidentally was the track used by the children to take food to the cave my father and Peter Gunn were hiding in. There was also a narrow tunnel under the road with an entrance at the top of steps on the other side. Living was on the first floor of the house with a small kitchen, a living room and Angela's bedroom. Three more bedrooms were on the second floor and there was an attic room, used by the escapees.

As to the PoWs, the villagers had little knowledge of how they fared, and they assumed that most of them died in the mountains or were killed while trying to escape. There are some buried at the war cemetery in Ortona. In a war journal the weather in the region in December is described as a combination of blizzards, drifting snow and poor visibility and this was in the area near Casoli so the difficulty that the villagers faced in the Majella was extreme and the chance of surviving the brutal cold of the high Majella was considered unlikely, which resulted in the villagers believing that the few PoWs who left in that direction had not survived.

Before the Germans occupied Pretoro the villagers were looking after thirteen English escapees which placed them in considerable danger of execution. They were short of food but were prepared to share what they had, and their sacrifice and bravery is an untold story. Even after they were forced out of their homes they continued to support escapees as best they could, but within a couple of weeks the writing was on the wall and it became a case of either making a break for it or surrendering. A number did give up and some had a go, either ending up in the cemetery in Ortona, getting recaptured, or successfully breaking through to the British line.

The evacuation of Pretoro in December 1943

There had been rumours in the village for a while that the Germans would occupy it, as its strategic location made it ideal for their headquarters. They had come into the village to assess various buildings for their use during the preceding month and it was most likely that they would evacuate all the villagers to a camp in Chieti or further north rather than allow them to stay. This gave the villagers a choice; move into a camp with an uncertain future, most probably facing starvation as supplies to the region dwindled, or vacate the village and move into the mountains. Some, possibly as many as 400, chose the latter, and began to prepare for it during November, moving food and livestock into caves high above the village. In early December the exodus began, quite slowly so as not to draw attention to it. Warm clothes, blankets, and feed for the livestock was carried daily up steep ravines to the secluded caves well hidden by dense forest of beech and fir. The weather was cooling rapidly with nightly temperatures falling below zero. It rained most days and low cloud would hang over the hills making it feel dank and unpleasant. The villagers were tough. Their daily lives were hard, and they were used to scratching their living from the soil, working from dawn to dusk and enduring life without the comforts we take for granted today. This resilience and refusal to bow to the will of the Germans says much of the character of these mountain people who are fiercely independent.

By the time the Germans came to occupy the village there remained only about 1,600, who were rounded up and shipped away to camps. The Germans established their headquarters in the house adjoining the Perseo house, using that as an annexe. These houses have magnificent views over the valley towards Rapino and would have given the Germans an excellent vantage for observation of the Gustav line and the Allied forces beyond. The Germans moved a battalion into the village and at its lower end built an ammunition dump near where the petrol station is today. They were none too happy to find that some villagers had cut and run, and spent some time trying to round them up to transport away to the camps in Chieti and the north. I assume their plan was to use Campo 21 now that it was empty of PoWs. They did capture quite a few of them but many were deep in the mountains in very difficult country and it was tough to track them down. After a half-hearted attempt they mostly gave up, save for a few excursions to loot for food and round up young men who they wanted for slave labour. However, there was constant danger from small patrols sent daily into the mountains to check on any Allied movements in the area.

The Germans kept a number of locals in the village to provide domestic services for them, such as cleaning, washing and cooking. These villagers provided a communication link for the cave dwellers and were able to syphon off a small quantity of German supplies to help feed their friends and family.

Maria Dimarines, who later married Verino Perseo, escaped the village with her family, including her grandparents, brother, cousins and mother. Her father was still away at war and had not been heard from for quite a while. They were soon captured while hiding in a cave and sent to Chieti with a number of other Pretoro people. An insider who worked in the camp knew them and aided their escape; I am not certain of the detail but was told by Verino's wife Maria that he managed to isolate the Pretoro people in one section of the camp and the next morning they escaped, moving to a house in Chieti for the night and then walking back to the mountains, a journey that took three days. Maria was seven at the time. Local families they met on the way back would give them food and shelter, either in their houses or sheds.

Life in the mountains was terribly hard. It was perishing cold, wet, and the caves dripped water. Up high there was snow in the mountains and frequently snow would fall lower in the valley. Their cave was at a height of 1,000 metres, so high enough for it to be freezing every night and only marginally warmer during the day. Cloud would be a constant companion bringing with it a biting dampness. They were able to forage for wood which was plentiful and spent much time huddled around fires. They slept on a bed of leaves and were always chilled. Food became very scarce and they were desperately hungry all the time. There was a constant fear of the Germans. They could be brutal and there was always great uncertainty about how one was going to be treated.

When in Pretoro I spoke with a villager called Silviano who gave me a feel for those times; and Angela D'Angelo, a young lady who lives in the village and had spent time teaching English in Glasgow, has provided further information on what went on.

One story Silviano imparted was the desperate struggle the villagers had preventing livestock from being plundered by the Germans. They had moved cattle deep into the mountains before the evacuation of the town and hidden them in concealed caves that were difficult to access. In January when daytime temperatures had fallen to well below freezing the villagers built a stone wall at the mouth of a cave being used to hide several cows and which connected to a larger cave that the villagers were using as their home. The villagers had built a fire in the cave but hadn't realised that the smoke was drifting through an aperture into the cave occupied by the cows, which were asphyxiated and died. While this was a disaster of major proportions it was alleviated by the freezing temperatures, as once the cows were skinned and gutted the meat was hung in the cave which acted like a giant freezer and kept the meat fresh. It did however mean they lost their supply of milk.

The Perseo family moved to a cave called 'Grotto di Baffone' and here they set up house. Because Angela Perseo owned and ran the grocers shop in the village she had had the foresight to store food in the cave and initially had a plentiful supply of dried fruits, oil, cheese, and flour to make bread which they shared generously with other people from the village. They also had a good supply of milk and meat from the cows and sheep that accompanied them. This cave had two levels, the livestock living 'downstairs' and the family above. Verino's wife Maria told me that her grandmother had cooked chickens and rabbits and had put them all in a sack, bringing this to the cave where it was stored in a very cold part of it. So initially survival was not that difficult. They had plenty of wood for the fire they kept permanently alight, and were able to build a cooking platform over the fire and construct a rudimentary oven to bake bread. They had stored fodder for the livestock and water was in abundance.

Unfortunately not all the villagers were loyal. Some still maintained fascist sympathies and they informed on the whereabouts of the livestock, probably for personal favour. The Germans were only too ready to loot so it became a game of cat and mouse; or the German Rex versus the Italian Pepino. The Perseos, like other families, divided their stock between caves, and it is just as well they did for soon after, their main cave was raided, and all livestock tethered were lost to the German enemy.

Maria Perseo recalled a terrifying ordeal she suffered when left alone in the cave after her mother and the elder children had gone further into the mountains to find a more secure cave to move to. After a few hours little Maria started to cry and left the cave to look for other people to shelter with until her mother returned. However, she met what she described as a bad man from Pretoro who she later learnt was an informer. He told her that she couldn't stay with his family, and added cruelly that her mother had been killed. Maria became desperate at this awful news and staggered away into the forest, sobbing uncontrollably. After a while she came across two German soldiers sitting on a rock smoking who mocked her in her distress. She then noticed behind a tall boulder her mother lying on the ground hiding from the Germans and who couldn't comfort her for fear of discovery. Had she been discovered the Germans would probably have taken her captive and sent her to the north of Italy, leaving her children to fend for themselves. Maria had the presence of mind to move away and wait for the Germans to leave, which they did after a while. Reunited with her mother, they moved soon after to a cave higher in the hills, but Angela did consider trying to get across the British lines at Casoli as they had little food left and she had five children to feed. This proved too treacherous an expedition to consider, so they clung onto their precarious existence.

Life became increasingly hard as the bitter cold of January descended from the high Abruzzo and each day felt more miserable than the previous one. They scratched a living from the forest, and many began to starve. The Germans were less visible in early 1944 as they seemed to have lost interest in coming into the hills of Majella, and the villagers supposed that pressure was mounting from the Allied front. Records as to the date of return to the village are scant and I assume it wasn't until late May 1944, which is when the Gustav Line was broken in the west of Italy. The Germans blew the ammunition dump situated in deep caves below the upper village to announce their departure. The explosion resulted in the destruction of a number of houses and a large section of mountainside.

The blowing of the dump killed Nicola Balerna who was hanging washing out at the time and was impaled by a piece of shrapnel.

Allied troops came into the village but didn't stay. The village and surrounding area had no strategic significance once the Germans had retreated, with the result that life returned to normal, albeit with much to do to rebuild their lives.

When the family returned to their home they had little food remaining, but Angela had been resourceful before she left and had hidden cooking oil and flour in almost inaccessible small caves near to the village. This was to prove invaluable as they struggled to feed themselves before the summer crop could be harvested.

There is little record of what happened to the many young men who were rounded up and shipped off to work in labour camps. Most of the civilians who lived in the Majella survived and returned to their homes. The villagers who were sent to northern Italy and Germany were mostly treated reasonably well and eventually returned home. There were a number of young people who were missing presumed dead as they never returned.

Angela Perseo deserves special mention. What an extraordinarily tough and resourceful woman she was. She was responsible for bringing up five children without help from her husband who had died, run a grocery business and organise the farming and preparation of much of the produce sold. Then in 1943 after the surrender of Italy she agreed to house two British escapees under the noses of the now occupying Germans. This was an enormous risk to take, as if discovered it would certainly have resulted in the loss of her livelihood and possibly her life, leaving the children as orphans.

In November 1943 she had to share her house with German officers, and even with this added burden and danger she determined that she would continue to supply food and wine to the two escapees now living in the cave, using her two young children as couriers.

Through all this she had the foresight to make plans for the family to leave the village and live in the mountains. She ferried food and livestock away from the village with farmhands acting as shepherds and she sought out caves that would provide the greatest shelter from the encroaching winter. By early December preparations had been made and the villagers who had decided this course started the exodus, quietly slipping away, but she had to remain at this time due to the German presence in her house. When she finally left, the whole family departed on the same morning, disappearing into the valley and away into the hills for several months of survival through the extremes of a viciously cold winter. She worked hard day and night to keep morale up, to look after her children and help organise the lives of the other villagers.

She continued to supply some food to the two escapees for a few more weeks, even though supplies were running dangerously low, showing again her determination and generosity of spirit. She was also prepared to share her stock with other villagers, acting in some respects as a mother to all. She deserves the highest praise and should have received some recognition for her gallantry in this forgotten theatre of war.

Verino inherited her strength of character and determination. From scratch he built a factory employing fifty townsfolk which he ran successfully for forty years.

I would like to salute them all and thank them for their extraordinary courage in the face of a brutal oppressor.

Acknowledgements

Rifle Brigade Chronicles 1940, 1941, 1942

Hastings, R.H.W.S., *The Rifle Brigade in the Second World War 1939–1945*, Gale (1950)

Mather, Carol, *When the Grass Stops Growing, A Memoir of the Second World War*, Pen & Sword (1997)

Lett, Brian, *An Extraordinary Italian Imprisonment, The Brutal Truth of Campo 21, 1942-3*, Pen & Sword (2014)

The BBC – Godfrey Talbot's despatch from Cairo in August 1942

Index